DARLING AMY

KATE SKYLARK & AMY VINCENT

Darling Amy

A Gripping True Story of Child Abuse,
Betrayal and a Mother's Neglect

Contents

A Note from Kate

My name is Kate Skylark. I fell into writing child abuse memoirs quite by accident after meeting Sophie Jenkins, co-author of my first book, *Dirty Little Dog*. And now, years later, *Darling Amy* will be the fifth book I have published in this series.

My intention in publishing these books is to provide a forum, a place that survivors of child abuse can be heard and believed, to gain closure and catharsis.

If you have a story to tell, just email kateskylark@outlook.com to find out about current publishing opportunities.

Darling Amy is a reader's story – just one of the many stories that are sent to me every week. Because it was so well written, I made the decision to make only small changes to the narrative. I wanted to preserve the raw feeling of Amy's story, not diluting the emotional impact by over-editing, or by trying to make the grammar perfect.

So, I have left it, for the main part, in Amy's own words. When you read the book, I think you will appreciate just why I chose to do this.

Chapter 1

When Hull was announced as the UK City of Culture for 2017, all I could do was laugh. It wasn't meant as any sort of insult to Hull because I live there and always have. What made me laugh, and after a while cry just a little, was the idea that thousands of people would be visiting my birth city to enjoy the street theatre and film festival, the art exhibitions, and live performances. Then they would disappear back along the M62 to wherever they came from with only pleasant memories of Hull.

That was never going to happen for me. My memories of Hull come in three packages, one set I'm creating now, one set from the age of fourteen to now, and another, darker, shameful set. I have worked hard over the years, to set these memories to one side, just so I don't live my life forever being bitter about those early years.

Any biographical story must start at some point in the person's life, and I've decided that those early years are where I'll begin. I hope that recounting those times will go some way to helping me put a lid on those memories for good …

Living on a council estate anywhere in the UK can be tough. Bad neighbours, rowdy youths, noise, the odd fight, especially at throwing out time at the local boozer. My life, on a council estate in Hull, was like a million other stories from across the nation and through the ages.

To me as a youngster, it all just seemed normal. That was life. All my friends played in the street, therefore so did I. From a very young age I learned enough street knowledge to make sure I stayed safe. Always on the lookout for cars so we could dodge back onto the grey, concrete slabs that made up the pavement. Always wary of any strange men or dodgy-looking types.

If it wasn't raining, my friends, my little sister Ivy and I would often go along to the little park at the end of the street where we would play on the swings and roundabouts. We always seemed to spend our time squealing at the top of our voices as one of the other kids would turn the roundabout as fast as they could. It was often a competition to see who could stay on it longest, before screaming that they were going to be sick.

I was always the one in the middle. Once I got to feeling too dizzy that would be me done. I would get off, then stagger away and find a bit of dry grass to lie down on until the sky stopped spinning around me.

Often, like I'd seen on the TV (when we were allowed to watch it) I'd lie back on the grass, feeling the warmth of the sun on my face. The rest of my friends would join me, and we would try to see things, shapes in the clouds that looked like elephants or rabbits. But I could never see anything, just big, white and grey fluffy lumps floating across the sky with the condensation trails from aeroplanes high above them, crisscrossing the sky on their way to who knows where.

I never really had much of an imagination as a kid. Maybe that was why I didn't see shapes in clouds. The other kids always seemed to be imagining a world way beyond the muck and grime we actually lived in. The boys, all action, playing cops and robbers, or soldiers, or spacemen.

The girls dreaming of princesses and fairy tales. They all really were in a world of their own.

For me? None of that stuff. I liked living in *this* life. I liked my sister. Loved her. I always, no matter what I was doing, kept an eye out for where she was and what she was up to. Or more importantly if anyone was doing anything to her. Back then, it was less about 'stranger danger', and more a case of making sure none of the local bullies were picking on her. If any of them did, then they knew that they were in trouble with me, when I arrived on the scene, the trouble stopped.

If you didn't stand up for yourself, the other kids would ride roughshod over you. Standing up for yourself might only have meant making sure you didn't miss your turn on the swings. But you soon came to realise that sticking up for yourself meant your place in the hierarchy was safe.

Parents? No. No parents supervising us most of the time. It was a free for all. In our area, we all knew each other anyway so not having a fretting parent nearby never seemed a problem. Having said that, sometimes, a stranger would just appear and wandered about of their own accord. But anybody, any grown-up who was hanging around and wasn't from the area was soon confronted by one of the mums or dads. So at least one or two of the parents must have been keeping an eye on us from behind the net curtains.

On the many occasions when it was raining, my sister and I would play in our backyard. We had an old coal shed out there that had long been abandoned from its original use. We used it as our den and, apart from the spiders, I loved that place.

I loved to read when I was a kid. So, Ivy and I would go to the library, which was only two streets away, and pick out four books each. We would read our books accompanied by the sound of rain drumming on the roof, and a single, slow drip where it had sprung a leak.

In the winter, when we weren't at school we would still play out. The best fun was when we would have a long icy stretch of pavement that we could make into a slide, each of us kids taking it in turn to see who could slide the furthest with one push, and without falling over. I lost count of the times I did fall over, grazing knees and elbows. But it was fun, and most importantly, it cost nothing. Because, like almost every household in the area, we were skint.

I have to say, my overriding memories of when I was a small child up to my teenage years were of freedom, friends, and fun. That is, at least when we were *outside*. When we were *inside* the story was somewhat different.

Chapter 2

I don't remember my dad. My mum never used to talk about him. From what I know, he came to Hull from Cornwall to join the fishing industry when times were tough down there. My nan lives in Cornwall so I guess that much might be true. But even she clammed up when I tried to talk to her about him. So I never did find out much about him.

I've given up trying to find out now. He has never been a part of my life, and was never around. So I have no feelings, one way or the other about him.

As far as I knew, all the kids I played with on the streets and in the park, were just the same as everyone else. Some of them had a dad on the scene, most of them didn't.

Most of the single mums had a boyfriend of sorts. There was one big group of blokes who seemed to flit from one woman to another at regular intervals, often leaving another baby waiting to be born a few months later.

The dads who *were* around were split between those who worked (who never seemed to be around much) and those on benefits (who also never seemed to be around much). The whole area was largely made up of what I would now call 'dysfunctional families' but back then, it was the norm. That was just how you lived your life.

What about my mum? Well I'm an adult now, and things are different, but when Ivy and I were just kids, she was just my mum. I had nothing to compare her to, and for most of my early life, I never considered for one minute whether she was a good or bad mum.

My mum also had a brother, Uncle Tony. He had moved off the estate, got a well-paid job, got married to Auntie Jo and they had a baby, Jason, my cousin. We didn't see them very often and when we did, we had to go over to their house on the bus. It took forever, and I always told my mum we should walk because it would be quicker, but she never listened.

When she was sober, my mum could actually be kind of lovely. Kind, funny and loving. The trouble was, her being properly sober only happened once in a blue moon. I don't know if she was a true alcoholic or not. I don't think I really understood the concept when I was kid. All I remember from the really early days is that my mum used to like to go out for a drink with her mates of an evening. Whenever she had enough money, that is exactly what she would do.

We would be packed off to a neighbour, Cheryl, who would let us sleep over for the night then drop us back at home the next morning. My mum even gave Cheryl a spare key, so she could let us in in the morning without having to knock. Cheryl would lock the door behind her when she left. Mum would still be in bed, where she would often stay for much of the day.

When money was tighter, my mum used to drink at home. Cheap vodka was her poison or, if she couldn't afford that, cans of cheap beer.

When she'd had a drink, she became a completely different person. She would shout and bawl, at us kids mainly, but she would also rage at the world and her life. She never used to throw stuff around (we didn't really have a lot worth throwing). But if Ivy and I happened to say something to annoy her, or do something noisy, particularly in the mornings, she might give us a slap. There was never any bruising or marks or anything like that. She would just lash out when she was pissed. We didn't like it, but we never thought much of it. If the slaps were the worst we ever had to suffer, that wouldn't make much of a story. If slaps were the worst of it, I wouldn't have written a whole book about my difficult childhood.

Occasionally a bloke would emerge from her bedroom on a Saturday morning. We knew most of them from the single mother merry-go-round and occasionally one of them would flip us a pound coin each and tell us to keep quiet about him being there. No doubt, many of these men were seeing a few different mums at the same time. And if they wanted to avoid trouble and fights, they needed to keep those women from finding out about each other.

I never would have said a word even without the reward, but I still took it. A pound each meant a trip to the local mini-mart for sweets. A rare treat indeed, and one that, whatever the weather, we always shared in the coal shed. You see, if my mum had seen us eating sweets, she'd have asked where we got the money from and why we didn't give it to her.

'You can't go buying sweets when I've got the leccy bill to pay!' she'd shout at us. We weren't allowed sweets, because she had so little money. But she'd have had a lot more spare cash if she hadn't spent so much on booze and fags.

Thinking back, I suppose my mum would be seen as neglectful to us kids now, but at the time that's just how it was. I'm sure there are all kinds of psychological explanations for her doing what she did. Neither of us thought anything of it because our friends mostly told similar stories, many considerably worse. So again, I don't really hold that against her.

And our house may have been tiny and poky, but despite all of my mum's troubles, she mostly kept the place neat and tidy, even if it wasn't always as sparkling clean as Uncle Tony's place.

The only thing I really didn't like back when I was little was that my mum smoked. A lot. I had seen all the warnings about health at school. I loved my mum and didn't want her to die of some horrible disease or another. But it wasn't just that. Her fag smoke stank and made me cough and my eyes water. It was really horrible.

Food was always an issue for me and Ivy. When my mum had been out for a night, we often had to make our own breakfast and lunch as she would lay in bed until her hangover had gone. Even when she drank at home, she never seemed to bother much with food. Money was always tight so whatever meals we did have were usually out of a tin. Beans, or tinned spaghetti. I actually don't remember my mum using the oven more than a handful of times right through my childhood. As we got older I encouraged Ivy to help me in the kitchen in case a day came when she didn't have me to get food for her.

But it was in the kitchen that the first really bad event took place, and my first really bad memory was formed. It was what happened in the kitchen one day that first made me start to worry about my mum, and whether we could trust her.

Chapter 3

It was a Saturday morning, and I remember coming out of my bedroom, the sun shining in through the grubby windows at the top of the stairs. It must have been springtime because our unheated house wasn't absolutely freezing cold. I would have been about twelve years old by then.

My mum had come in late, way past midnight. Although they tried to be quiet, she (and whoever the bloke was she brought back) had kept me awake with grunting and moaning.

I tried to block it out and go to sleep. But I ended up just reading a book until it quietened down and was replaced by gentle snoring. It seemed like hours I had lain awake.

I jumped awake the next morning to the sound of our front door slamming closed. My mum's bedroom door was slightly open as I walked past so I poked my head around to make sure she was okay. It wouldn't have been the first time she came home drunk and woken up with a black eye with no idea who had given it to her. Before I went in I caught a whiff of the smell coming from her bedroom. It was horrible: fags, beer, sweat, they were all there. But there was also a musky smell of body odour mixed with a thick, almost salty smell I didn't recognise. It all combined to give off a musty stink that caught at the back of my throat. It made me feel sick and want to cough.

'You OK, Mum?' I whispered.

No response, not even a grunt.

I took a couple of steps away, took in a lungful of fresher air, then went back to the room, pushing the door a little wider with a little squeak.

'Mum, are you okay?' I spoke to her while trying not to breathe, which is no easy task.

I crept around to her side of the bed and slid back the covers from over her face. She didn't move other than to twitch a little where the cold, morning air started to cool her skin.

She very quietly murmured something, but I couldn't make out what it was. Her face was fine, no bruises. When I looked at her, the bright morning light illuminating her face, I realised for the first time just how old she had started to look. She must have only been about thirty-two at the time. The brightness from the window highlighted every little crease and crevice as well as the first few broken blood vessels around her cheeks. She still had on the makeup she had put on the night before, but the mascara had run to make dark patches under her eyes that almost hid her natural dark patches. The lipstick she'd had on was almost all gone but an outline of dark lipliner remained.

'This is my mum,' my twelve-year-old brain said, 'and she looks like a dead person on the TV.'

Until then she had just been Mum, but I was growing up and starting to understand a bit more about the world in general. I knew a woman in her early-thirties shouldn't look like that, even after a night out drinking.

I I was definitely growing up, although I'm not sure that my mum had noticed. You see, I remember that morning distinctly because my periods had started that morning. I had woken up to find a bit of blood in my knickers. Nothing unusual there, I now know. But I still needed someone to talk to about it, to reassure me that what was happening to me was normal, to give me what I needed to cope. In short, I *needed my mum*. But looking down at her that morning as she finally pulled the covers back up over her face, I knew that whatever I needed, I wasn't going to get it from her.

I walked out of her bedroom and quietly pulled the door closed behind me. I could feel tears welling up at the idea that I was being left alone to face this big change within me. I went into the bathroom, took one of my mum's sanitary towels, and put it in my knickers. I don't remember ever talking to my mum about whether or when my periods started. Not then, or in the future.

Ivy came out of her room just then, bleary-eyed, and with her hair in a mess.

'You okay, Amy?' she whispered. We'd both been taught by multiple slaps to stay as quiet as possible when Mum was sleeping off a night out.

I forced a smile onto my face for my little sister. 'Yeah I'm fine. Mum's sleeping. She came in late last night.'

She nodded. She was as used to this situation as I was. She didn't even look concerned. I suppose, like for me, this sort of thing had happened too often for it to be anything out of the ordinary.

'I'm hungry.' She was stick thin, without an ounce of excess flesh on her body. Like me, Ivy rarely had enough to eat. My own body had started to curve in places, but I was also thinner than I should have been.

'Let's get some breakfast,' I said with a smile.

'Okay.' She grabbed me, linking arms and, trying not to giggle too loudly, we went downstairs.

Once we were down the stairs, Ivy headed into the living room to switch on the TV. I walked down the hall to shut the front door. When Mum's night-time companion had slammed it behind him, it must have not caught on the latch. I pushed it to, noticing that the sky in the distance had darkened. It was going to rain.

I went back down the hallway and into the kitchen. When I opened up the food cupboard, it was almost empty. Mum hadn't been shopping for over a week, bar a trip to the local corner shop every day to stock up on fags. There was a half loaf of bread. That was going to have to do for breakfast.

In the fridge there was not much more. Four cans of beer, an almost empty pot of jam and the scrapings of a pack of spreadable butter. It would have to do.

Ten minutes later I went into the living room to find Ivy engrossed in The Simpsons. I plonked a plate of toast and jam on the centre seat of the sofa. I went back into the kitchen and came back with two glasses of tap water. The fridge hadn't run to any milk and we were down to the last teabag, so no tea that morning for us two.

While I fetched the water, Ivy had quickly run upstairs and brought down her duvet. Although it wasn't freezing cold outside, it was still a bit chilly inside the house. While I had been making the toast, the first few spots of rain had started hitting the kitchen window.

When she got back we both curled up on the sofa, covered ourselves with the duvet and set to munching our way through the toast. I'd made six slices. I got through two of them while Ivy had eaten her three. When she'd finished her third she looked up at me with her gorgeous brown cow eyes, without saying a word.

'Go on then,' I said, rolling my eyes at her. She didn't need a second invitation and a minute later the extra slice of toast with a thin scraping of spread and jam had disappeared never to be seen again.

We watched the TV for hours. It made a nice change to be able to watch what we wanted, rather than the game shows and chat shows Mum used to have on all day. Because she was in bed, the room wasn't full of fag smoke, so not being able to go out and play seemed less of a problem.

Ivy and I sat on the sofa, wrapped up warm in the duvet, and we talked. We talked about everything. TV shows we liked. TV shows we didn't like. Stuff that had happened at school. Teachers. Everything. And most of the time we laughed, happy to be warm and have full bellies, even if it was only toast and jam. We were really close as sisters. We still are.

We even played games. We didn't have a games console which hurt a bit when some of the other kids bragged about their PlayStations, but we still played games – everything from I-Spy to hangman. Anything you could play in your head or on a piece of paper.

It was the best time.

Outside the rain came down steadily.

We had what my mum called her money box in the kitchen. Whenever she had spare change in her coat pocket or her purse, she would sort out the coppers and the odd bit of silver, and put it in this old ice cream box. Then it would just sit there.

Come the middle of the afternoon, Ivy and I were both hungry again. Mum was still asleep upstairs. I'd heard her get up and go to the toilet earlier on and wondered if she might come down. When she came out the smell of cigarette smoke came out with her and drifted downstairs, but she just went back to bed.

I knew there wasn't enough food in to even make a sandwich and I didn't want Ivy to go hungry. So, I went into the kitchen and emptied Mum's money box quietly out on the counter, and started to count it out into little piles of coins.

There was just over three pounds and fifty pence there. This was a fair sum of money. I made a small shopping list in my head. Milk. A loaf of white sliced bread. A cheap tub of buttery spread. A jar of beef paste. The smallest box of teabags. £3.65 or somewhere close. With a bit of luck, the owner of the shop would let me owe the difference.

'Ivy,' I whispered through from the kitchen. 'I'm going to the shop to get some stuff for our tea.

Listen out for mum and if she shouts, make sure she knows you are here. Okay?'

Ivy nodded. She was more than capable of looking after herself for ten minutes.

I pulled on my grubby school coat, quietly opened the front door and stepped out. Outside, for once, the streets were quiet. Head down, I walked quickly to the mini-mart. It was still teeming with rain as it had been all day. The local kids were at home, annoying their parents no doubt. I knew one or two would be coming to school on Monday with new bruises. It was always the same after a wet weekend.

When I got to the shop, I took my time getting my stuff. I needed to tot up the bill as I went along. Last thing to get was the milk. I'd found a loaf that was marked down because it was yesterdays 'best before' date. The spread was on offer too so I got the lot for £3.10 by my reckoning. When I got to the front of the queue, I lifted up the basket onto the counter.

On the top of the counter were the small impulse buy bars of chocolate. 10p each would get me and Ivy a Chomp bar. A rare treat.

I piled up small handfuls of change on the counter, to hear much tutting from the old lady behind me in the queue. While the man counted the change into pounds I waited. When he got close to the right amount I loaded the stuff into my carrier bag and waited again. I *so* wanted there to be 20p left over so I could buy myself and my sister the smallest treat in the shop, a bar of chocolate covered toffee.

'How much is left?' I asked when the shopkeeper had taken what he needed.

He counted through the copper coins.

'15p love. You want something else?'

I can't describe the feeling of disappointment that flooded over me, all over a bar of chocolate.

'Two Chomps, please,' I said, pointing at the box on the counter.

The shopkeeper looked at me and then at the box. I wanted to cry. When I look back now it feels a bit silly, but I so wanted to surprise Ivy. I knew a treat like that would brighten up the day for both of us.

'Here, love.' A voice from behind me.

I turned to face the old lady who had been tutting. She was holding out a shiny silver 5p piece. I held out my hand and took it from her, shyly. I could only manage a whisper and a blush when I said, 'Thanks, Mrs Bradley. I'll give it back soon.'

'I don't want it back, love. I've been where you are now, and people helped me out back then.'

'Okay, well, thanks anyway. I will bring it back.'

I slid the coin across the counter, grabbed the two chocolate bars, dropped them in the bag, and left as quickly as I could. My face was scarlet and hot. I was embarrassed, of course, to be taking the old lady's money. But when I think about it now all these years later I realise that it was a tiny amount of money. (I posted a coin back through Mrs Bradley's door a week later.)

When I got back to the house, Ivy came straight to the door.

'I'm glad you're back. Mum just shouted down for a cup of tea. I said you were in the toilet. Come on.'

She nearly dragged me into the kitchen. She had already filled up the kettle which was rumbling to a boil as I started to unload the goodies from the shop. I left out the milk and teabags while Ivy set up two more mugs for the two of us. I know kids are supposed to like squash and fizzy drinks but we both loved a cup of tea.

I put the bread, spread, and beef paste on the worktop ready to make sandwiches as the kettle clicked off behind me. I was really looking forward to mine. I was starving hungry again. Then I grabbed the two precious chocolate bars and turned to show them to Ivy.

'Look what I got,' I said with a beaming smile on my face, embarrassment forgotten for now.

Ivy had been making tea by herself for a long while, and knew what she was doing. But for some reason that day, she got it wrong. Instead of turning her head to look at me and our surprise treat, she swung her whole body around, kettle in hand, steaming, hot, scalding water still pouring from the spout.

Almost as if it was slow motion, I saw the boiling water hit her. Most of the water hit her dressing gown which soaked up most of the water, leaving it hot but harmless. More water hit the floor. But the last, steaming spout of boiling water arched down and landed on her bare right foot.

She screamed.

Chapter 5

That is one sound that will live with me forever. My little sister lying on the floor of our kitchen in a pool of steaming water holding her foot and screaming at the top of her voice. The kettle, on its side, was glugging its contents slowly across the floor.

My first reaction was to freeze. For a second or two the noise echoing through the tiny kitchen was deafening. I just stood, watching Ivy, her hair all wet now and screaming my name.

I ran. I thundered up the stairs, smashed through my mum's door, banging it back against the wall.

'What the fuck ...' she mumbled from beneath the covers. 'Where's my tea? What's that noise?'

I grabbed the covers and pulled them, but she wouldn't let go.

'There's been an accident, Mum. Ivy has spilt boiling water on her foot and is screaming the house down.'

My mother groaned under the covers. I tried to pull them again. She still wouldn't let go.

'Okay, okay, I'll be down in a minute. Go and put some cold water in a bowl and tell Ivy to put her foot in it.'

I ran as fast as I could back down the stairs. Why hadn't I thought of that? I'd watched all the safety films at school. I should have known what to do about burns and all that.

'And don't forget to make my tea,' Mum shouted as I ran.

When I got to the kitchen, Ivy had stopped screaming but was now sobbing, crying that her foot hurt and was burning. I helped her to get up. 'Come on, Ivy,' I said as I helped her hop through to the living room and sat her down on the couch. I needed to go get the bowl, but she was clinging onto me and wouldn't let me go.

'Mum said I've got to get you to put your foot in some cold water, Ivy. Let me go.' I pulled her hands off me and ran to the kitchen. Ivy's voice, calling out my name, was ringing in my ears as I went.

Filling up the bowl seemed to take ages. I opened the tap up as wide as it would go but time seemed to have slowed down. The bowl filled so slowly, it seemed like the longest few minutes of my life. Once it was full enough, I turned off the tap and tried to pick it up. I never realised before just how heavy a large quantity of water can be. In the end I managed to get it out of the sink and through to the living room, but only by slopping lots of it on the floor.

I put the bowl down on the carpet by Ivy, so she could put her foot in the water. The whole of her foot had turned bright red and was hot to touch. I gently lowered it into the cold soothing water then jumped up on the sofa to give Ivy a hug.

She was still crying so I stayed there, gently rocking her in my arms, as my own tears started to fall. My heart was pounding away. When Ivy started to shiver, I grabbed the duvet and wrapped us up in it.

It was all because of me. If I hadn't done the whole surprise chocolate thing, she wouldn't have whipped around, and the water would have gone where it was meant to go – in the mugs and not on her tiny white foot.

After what felt like forever but was probably more like ten minutes, I heard the sound of footsteps clumping down the stairs. By this time Ivy had calmed down a bit and was just crying. The yelling and screaming had stopped.

'Who's spilt all this water on the floor?' was the first thing Mum asked as she went into the kitchen. 'Amy, come and wipe up this mess.' I heard her pick up the kettle and start to refill it.

'I can't. I'm in here looking after Ivy.'

'Oh, right. I suppose I'll have to do it myself then.' I could hear her mumbling and muttering to herself in the kitchen. She still hadn't even poked her head in to see how Amy was.

'What's all this stuff in here?' she shouted through.

I swore silently to myself. I'd left all the food I'd bought out on the worktop. She was bound to ask where I got the money.

'I went to the shop to get you some tea, Mum. We'd run out and we'd got no milk either. I took some change out of the money box. Is that alright?'

The sound of the kettle rumbling filtered through the kitchen door and Ivy held on tighter, whimpering in my ear. I was scared, waiting for one of my mum's explosive temper outbursts to come my way. Instead, all I could hear was her grumbling to herself about having to clean up after us and make her own tea.

When she finally shuffled through the doorway into the living room she hardly even glanced over at us on the sofa. Ivy had her head buried in my lap, now producing the occasional sniff and sob. Her foot was still under the cold water. I was wide-eyed, waiting for the telling off and slap I felt sure was coming.

My mum put her tea down on the little table next to her favourite chair and stood back up, looking at the TV for a moment or two before turning her gaze on us.

'Come on. Let's have a look then. Show me the damage,' she sounded bored.

I nudged Ivy. 'Take your foot out and show Mum,' I said.

Ivy whimpered a bit but slowly lifted her foot out of the water, drops falling back into the bowl with tiny splashes. I couldn't see Ivy's foot properly from where I was sitting, but the moment Ivy lifted it out of the water my mum swore.

'Why didn't you come and get me sooner?' she said.

'Mum, I came and got you as soon …'

She wasn't listening. I could see in her face that she was worried. As it turns out she was worried more for herself than for either of us.

I leaned forward to see what had made my mum go pale. Ivy's foot was bright red, it had already started to swell up, and a huge blister was popping up. It looked really bad.

'Shouldn't we go to the doctor's, Mum?'

'No!' She snapped out the word so forcefully that I jumped back a bit.

'Why?' I managed to ask in a quiet voice.

'Because if we do they'll start asking questions. About how it happened.' She looked over at me, with a mixture of anger and fear. 'If they start asking questions and don't like the answer, they'll probably tell the social. You know what they're like. They'll put me away. Do you want me to go to prison?' Then she added, 'They'll end up taking you off me. You don't want that, do you?'

Although I didn't really understand what was going on at the time, we'd had contacts with Social Services before. From what I can remember somebody expressed concern about us because we were so thin. We'd had a social worker for a little while but eventually she stopped coming. That's all I can remember about that. Janice. That was the social worker's name. She asked a lot of questions. That had been a few years previously and it hadn't been a big deal at the time. Most of the kids on my street had been involved with the social at one time or another so nobody batted an eye when we were.

But my mum saying that they might take us away *was* a big deal. I had heard of this happening before with other families. Some kids ended up in foster homes, or worse, children's homes.

Ending up in a children's home was a massive fear for me. I didn't want to get taken away. I actually liked it at home. I loved Ivy. I even loved my mum and my house. At that moment, I agreed with my mum – the doctor was a seriously bad idea.

'What are we going to do?' I asked.

I'd never seen my mum looking so serious. 'Let me think a minute. Put your foot back in the water, Ivy.' Mum went and sat in her chair and lit up a cigarette. I could smell it immediately and what with the scare and the idea of going into care, the stink of it made me feel even sicker.

'Ivy? You'll have to stay off school. I'll write a note. You can take it on Monday, Amy.' I nodded. 'I'll say she has got gastric flu or something.' She looked up from her tea. 'You need to make sure you keep your mouth shut.'

I nodded. I'd do anything to avoid being taken away.

So that's what we did. On the Monday, my mum was up in time to write me a note which I delivered to the school office. I read it on the way in that Monday, just so I knew what to say if anybody asked. I kept my mouth shut about what really happened.

I knew that once you started talking about kids having the trots and puking 24/7 teachers and school staff were generally accepting. Besides Ivy and I actually had decent school records. We went every day and weren't any trouble. Well, no more than the average kid anyway.

Gastric flu was what Mum wrote in her shaky handwriting, so gastric flu it was. It was nearly two weeks until Ivy came back. I know the school were starting to get twitchy by then, because they kept asking me about her.

Ivy never did get taken to the doctor, and today the skin on top of her right foot is still all scarred and discoloured

You know, there is a saying that every cloud having a silver lining, although sometimes it's hard to see. But this episode really did have a silver lining.

For the next six months or so, Mum barely drank at all. She cooked, she cleaned, she even got herself a cash in hand job working at the pub as a cleaner. For a while, everything about life was great.

Chapter 5

It was a conversation I had one day with Mr Rajesh, the man who owned the mini-mart, that made me start thinking about what I wanted from life.

Mum had sent me up to the shop to buy milk again. Nobody else was in the shop and Mr Rajesh had just taken the milk from me to beep it through his till.

'Are you looking forward to going back to school, Amy?'

Although I was kind of tough with other kids, I was shy with adults and not used to talking to them in any kind of normal way. So I just shrugged an 'I don't know' face. Mr Rajesh had a broad Hull accent. Even though he was Asian.

'Listen. You are a good kid, Amy. You say 'please' and 'thank you' and don't come into my shop and steal things. I know it isn't 'cool' to work hard at school but ask yourself this – Do you still want to be living around here in ten years' time? You only get one chance of doing well at school. Don't throw it away.'

I took the milk, shrugged again, and said thank you, then I walked home. I never gave it a second thought until one weekend we went over to see my uncle Tony. Just to spend some time in a house where there was no fag smoke was a huge treat. Walking into their house was like breathing in country fresh air all the time. The only thing it smelled of a bit was cleaning products and air freshener.

My mum always grumbled when we went to Tony's because she had to go out into the garden to smoke. I remember wishing she would do that at home too. But I would never dare say it.

My uncle's house was so different from ours. It had a front garden, with a lawn, close-trimmed and tidy. It had a shiny car on the front drive, an Audi, I think. The windows were clean and the UPVC was shiny and white, inside and out. The windows had venetian blinds instead of ragged old curtains that didn't meet in the middle. There was a dining table and they ate their meals at this table every day. I can remember looking at this table, wondering how the wood could shine so much in the light from the window. I loved sitting at the shiny table to eat. At home, we only ever ate meals on our laps in front of the TV.

Tony's house was like being in another world for me and Ivy. For a start, Tony always made sure we had plenty to eat. But that wasn't all. His house made ours look like a slum. Looking at it now, Tony's place was just a house in a suburb of Hull. It really wasn't anything special at all, in the grand scheme of things. But to me it was like being one step from heaven. This place was really was like a paradise compared to home

The stairs had thick, plush carpet on them rather than bare wood. The hallway walls had mirrors and paintings or prints on them and each light fitting had a matching lampshade instead of bare bulbs with cobwebs hanging all around them.

When I opened the bathroom door and pulled on the light switch cord, the whole room lit up so brightly I thought a flash had gone off. Every surface gleamed and sparkled. Bright white tiles and mirrors on the wall gave the whole room a clean look that our dull bathroom at home could never have. Tony's bathroom even had a separate shower!

When I first saw Jason's bedroom, I almost wanted to cry. It was a perfect nursery. There was a mural painted on one wall of farmyard animals. Fluffy carpet was on the floor. The cot bed had a mobile hanging above it. And next to the cot was a nightlight that shone stars onto the ceiling.

That particular day, we were all out in the back garden. Uncle Tony and Auntie Jo were letting their little boy, Jason, have a bit of a toddle around. He was only about two at the time, so he kept falling over but laughing at the same time. I loved Jason. He was so cute when he was little.

When he disappeared for a moment behind the garden shed, Auntie Jo went off to find him, leaving my uncle and I alone on the garden bench.

We had just eaten a lovely roast lunch. The sun was shining down, and I closed my eyes and turned my face up to catch the rays. I could hear crows cawing in the distance and the closer sound of a small bird singing merrily away. The air was full of the smell of barbecues cooking in nearby gardens.

'It's so nice here,' I said. 'I want to live in a place like this.'

'You could if you wanted to,' Uncle Tony said.

My uncle was a tall man, with a deep voice that sounded smooth, not like my mum's voice which was harsh and rasping from too many fags. I looked at him. He had a cup of coffee in his hand, watching Auntie Jo and Jason as they messed about down at the bottom of the garden.

'How?'

'Work hard at school, Amy. It's the best chance you'll ever have to get yourself a good life.'

I thought about that for a moment then told him about what Mr Rajesh had said to me. Tony smiled and nodded like he wasn't surprised. Then he turned and sat up a bit on the bench, so he could look at me properly.

'Mr Rajesh is a good bloke, Amy. You should listen to him. He said the same thing to me you know?'

'Did he?'

I was amazed. My future wasn't something I had ever talked about with Mum. If I had she probably would have laughed at the idea of me doing anything worthwhile with my life.

'He did,' Tony carried on explaining how Mr Rajesh had helped him. 'He told me it was my only chance and not to throw away my life. It took me a while, but I started to pay attention at school, not a moment too soon either. I used to look at some of the other families and wonder if I wanted to spend my life on the dole, scraping around for a few quid to be able to eat. That wasn't what I wanted and him saying that made me realise that school was the best chance I had of getting out of there.'

'What did you do.'

'Got my head down and grafted. I took every extra lesson that was on offer. I started to read instead of watching the telly at night. I did a few odd jobs around the estate too, so I had a bit of my own money'

'What happened then?'

'Well, after a while the teachers saw what I was doing and started to help me when they could. I mean most of the time they were chasing around after the kids who thought it was a good idea to mess about and disrupt the lessons. So, I used to get them to set me tests I could do after school, and point me in the right direction for the stuff I got wrong. You know, stuff I didn't know? In the end I passed all my exams, then I went to college where I did even more exams and passed them. Then I started applying for jobs, got this job and worked weekends until Jo and I got the money together for a deposit on this place. I love it here too, you know?'

He made it sound so easy. I didn't say anything else. I just nodded and watched my mum, scowling at Jason and stubbing out another fag.

***

From that day, I resolved to follow in my uncle Tony's footsteps, and to take Mr Rajesh's advice. I would do whatever I could to make sure I didn't end up staying on our estate. I wanted a house like Tony's, and I would do whatever I could to get it.

There was a sort of unwritten rule in our school that governed where you sat in class. Kids from the posh estate near the school all used to sit at the front. In the middle of the class were the kids from my estate. Right at the back were the real troublemakers.

I used to watch the posh kids from my desk. They all had new uniforms, nice shoes and their hair was always smartly cut. Mine was always pulled back into a ponytail to keep it tidy. School uniform was expensive and inevitably, Ivy and I ended up with stuff that other kids had outgrown. Their mums would flog them off for whatever they could get, and it always seemed to be us who ended up with a blazer that was too big, smelled bad, and had all sorts of weird stuff in the pockets. The ties we had often had ink blots.

The kids from the posh estates would come to school in nice new stuff every year, brand new shoes, shirts, and trousers. Ivy and I, and a lot of other kids from our area, came in whatever we could get. I might have had a scruffy uniform, but that wasn't going to stop me.

I decided I was going to sit at the front of the class from now on.

The first time I sat myself at the front of the class, I got a lot of funny looks. There was some tittering amongst the posh kids, but no one stopped me. Mrs Abbott, the teacher, just said, 'Are you going to be alright there, Amy?' But I was fine. I had a plan, and no one was going to stop me carrying it out.

I just sat there, quietly, trying my best to understand what was on the whiteboard and what the teacher was saying.

I had never spoken to my teachers, outside of answering the odd question. But with what Mr Rajesh and Uncle Tony had said to me, I decided it was time to set my life in order. If this was my only chance to get a house like Tony's, I was going to grab it with both hands. It was time to ask for help.

When the bell rang, I fiddled about with my bag, dropped my stubby pencil and half-full pen on the floor, and tied and retied my shoelaces until every other kid left the room, then I gathered up my stuff and walked up to the teacher's desk.

Mrs Abbott was looking down, marking some books and didn't look up.

'Miss,' I said

'Mmm-hmm.'

I was really nervous. I hadn't really thought through what I wanted to say before I'd gone up there and now I was tongue-tied. Mrs Abbott was still head down.

'I need some help, Miss. I want … I want … to pass my exams.'

Slowly she lifted her eyes up from her marking. For a few moments she said nothing, just looked at me. Maybe she was trying to work out if I was just winding her up, I don't know, but in the end, she spoke.

'What do you need?'

I coughed to clear my tight throat.

'Some tests I can do after school.' She nodded. 'And some help to find out about the stuff I get wrong.' She looked at me again. She didn't wear glasses, but I bet if she had she'd have been looking over the tops of them at me. I started to feel a bit uncomfortable. But in the end, she nodded again. Then she leaned over, slid a drawer of her desk open and pulled out a folder. She opened it on her desk, thumbed through some of the papers in there and slid one out. It was made up of several sheets stapled together. She looked it over, then slid it across the table to me.

'Bring it back when you've done it,' she said.

'Thank you,' I said, picking it up. 'I will.'

And that was it. From then on, I did the same in every lesson, except art. I have no imagination and couldn't draw or paint anything that didn't look like a toddler or a trained chimp had done it, so art was a lost cause for me.

For months, I religiously completed all the teachers gave me. By following the good advice from a couple of people and showing a bit of willing, I might just manage to create a future far away from the grubby rooms and litter-strewn streets of my childhood.

With Mum on the wagon and me working hard at school, the future was looking rosy.

Chapter 6

One of the big things that used to make me feel sad at school was summer holidays.

Talk about a tale of two cities.

The posh kids would come back full of tales about being taken to France or Spain and in some cases Florida for a holiday and often I would sit and listen to them talking and wonder what it would be like to travel. The stories they would tell about visiting places would have me daydreaming about going to places like that. Feeling a hot sun on my back. Eating exotic food. Seeing things we had only ever seen on TV.

The summer after Ivy's accident, we finally managed a holiday ... of sorts. I mentioned before that my Nan lived in Cornwall. Well, that summer she arranged for us to go and see her down there.

Mum, Ivy and I set off one Saturday morning at the crack of dawn. We walked into the city centre and caught the coach just after seven in the morning. It was probably the most exciting thing I'd ever done. I was mesmerised by everything as we travelled, from the big cities we travelled through to the quiet farms as we passed on the motorway. There was so much green everywhere. We had to change coaches in Birmingham which gave my mum a chance to chain smoke. While she smoked, Ivy and I ate the jam sandwiches we had bought with us. We were just sitting on a bench in the bus station at Birmingham surrounded by diesel fumes, but it still felt like an adventure.

When we got on the next coach we imagined it would only be a couple of hours to the coast. Six hours later we finally pulled into the bus station in Plymouth. It had taken twelve hours in total to get there.

My nan had arranged to pick us up from the bus station and drive us the rest of the way. It was great to see my nan again. It had been a long time since the last time I saw her, and she looked older. Her hair was greyer than it had been, but she seemed younger than my mum. After we had both given her a huge hug, and she had said how big we had both grown, we made it back to the car and piled in.

When we got out of the city centre, my mum asked if she could light up. But Nan just said, 'No, love. Not with the kids in the car.'

I asked Nan how long it would take to get to hers and Mum groaned when Nan said 'a couple of hours'. Inwardly, I groaned too. Exciting as the travelling had been, it had a long day. I just wanted to get out, have something to eat (I was starving by then), and stretch my legs. In the end we got to the little village where she lived just before 9 p.m. Nan drove into the centre of the village and parked the car.

'Come on girls, I'm going to treat you,' Nan said, walking off. We followed her, excited to know what the treat would be. Eventually, we reached it. The Fish and Chip shop.

Ten minutes later the four of us were sitting on the harbour wall, our backs to the town, looking out at the sea and eating the most delicious thing I'd eaten in months. A piece of cod in batter and a generous helping of chips, with lashings of salt and vinegar, and a can of fizzy drink. Each!

Ivy and I just kept looking at each other as we devoured the food. I was happy, smiling at her, and she had the biggest grin I have ever seen on her face.

We never, ever, had takeaway at home. It cost too much, even when Mum was making a bit of extra cash on the side and was not drinking much. And if we *had* ever had takeaway, it would probably have been one portion between the three of us.

All I could hear was the sound of chewing, the rustle of paper packaging, and the gentle rush of the sea against the harbour wall. When I looked up I could see the stars in the sky. Even though the street was lit, it was a gentle light, not like the masses of orange lights at home in Hull that made the night sky look like daytime.

The smell of the fish and chips was so delicious, it almost made me wish I lived over a chip shop. At least that smell would be better than fag smoke. Just as I thought that, mum lit up.

By the time we got back to Nan's house it was well gone ten. The early start, the lengthy journey and a very full belly meant I could barely keep my eyes open.

That was, until I got out of the car.

Where Nan lived was in the back of beyond. Her house backed on to fields and hills. There was no other house anywhere to be seen and no streetlights. I grabbed my stuff out of the boot and stepped back so I didn't crack my head when the boot was closed. That was when I looked up. It was incredible. A sight I will carry with me in my head forever.

The sky was pitch black. The moon was a thin sliver just above the horizon. And sparkling up in the sky were more stars than I ever imagined existed. At home you'd be lucky to see more than the brightest stars but in my nan's garden, I could see them all. From the tiniest pinpricks of silver light, to bright shining stars that twinkled and seemed to be changing colour as I watched them. It's was the most awesome thing I had ever seen in my life.

While we were there, it became a nightly thing for me to go out and sit in my nan's garden and stare at the starts. Sometimes, I'd lie down on the grass. It was one of those times, like when you stand on top of a mountain (yes, I have done that), that makes you realise just how small we really are, and how much is out there that we just don't know about.

The week we spent at Nan's was, by a long way, the best week I could remember. Every day we would go off in the car to visit all sorts of places that cost nothing other than a parking fee. My nan would get up and make proper sandwiches. And, straight after breakfast, we would just go off for the day. One of my favourite places was a small beach not too far away. It was a bit of a climb down the cliffs but when we got down there it was like being in another world. Even on a sunny day, in the height of the season there were no more than handful of other people on the beach at any one time.

It was just so different to home that we could have been on another planet. Warm sun, breaking waves, rock pools to explore. There was even a cave, but we were too scared to do any more than stand at its entrance, in case a horde of cutlass waving pirates came rushing out. Silly, I know, but we were both still only kids. This was something so wildly outside of our normal life that I think we could be forgiven for being just a bit overawed by the whole thing.

Even mum seemed to enjoy herself. Although she didn't seem to like having to walk back up the cliff path. We would have to stand and wait for her to catch up as she wheezed along.

That whole week was magical. We had seen and done so many things that we never could do at home. It opened my eyes to what there was out there in the big wide world away from the dull grey streets in Hull. It was with great sadness, and a determination to come back again soon, that we climbed into Nan's car on Sunday morning, to start the long journey home.

By the end of the summer holidays I was even more determined to do well at school. It was the only way I could get a life like Tony's and Nan's. Mum had been laying off the booze a lot for a good few months and that summer is one I remember with great fondness. I felt like we were a proper family. I felt like I belonged to something good.

But the happiness was to be short-lived. Not long after we went back to school, things took a dramatic change.

Chapter 7

'Mum, Mum! I got my Maths test results back today,' I shouted as I walked in through the back door of the house that Friday.

I was incredibly excited. Maths had always been a bit of a struggle for me but with the extra work I'd been putting in, and with the help of a very patient teacher, I'd started to make some real progress. Instead of being near the bottom of the class, in this test, I'd come second. Although I tried not to show it in class, I was incredibly proud of myself.

When Mr Jacobs, my maths teacher, read out the results, I got some weird looks. The posh kids all looked at me as if an alien had just walked into the room. The other kids looked confused. Here was Amy, the scruffy kid from the rough estate, beating almost all of them in a test. It was unheard of. The only kid who beat me was the resident maths genius Archie Brown. He looked at me with a smile I couldn't read. Either he liked the idea that he might have some competition to start to push him a little, or he was gloating that he was still the best at maths.

The kids behind me, most of whom lived in the same area as me, either looked puzzled, wondering how I managed such a great result, or were glaring at me. They were probably readying their break time insults, ready to call me a 'swot' or some such nonsense. I took absolutely no notice of them, any of them. I was taller than all the other girls and most of the boys at that time, and my reputation for taking no nonsense from the street was well known, so nobody dared say anything to my face. There were mutterings from both groups, but I didn't care. I wasn't working hard and doing all that extra work for them or for anybody else. I was doing it for me, so that I had a future. So that I could have a house with carpet on the stairs, a separate shower, and an Audi on the drive.

I was so excited to tell my mum about the test. Perhaps she'd be just a little bit proud of me.

'Mum?' I shouted up the stairs. Sometimes, mum did a bit of ironing in her bedroom. Maybe she was up there. No reply.

That's when I heard it. A sound coming from the living room. A sound I hadn't heard for months. As soon as I heard it, I knew that the glorious intermission we had been enjoying was over. For a long time, life had been on the up. But how, I knew it was on the slippery slope back down. Even then, I had no idea just how far into the gutter we all were all going to end up. If I'd known what was eventually going to happen, I would have run far away, right at that moment. I'd have dragged Ivy with me, and never looked back.

The sound, was my mum, humming to herself. That sound has haunted me for years. Even now I can't abide the sound of anybody humming, even if (unlike with my mum) it is in tune.

I looked over at Ivy and the downcast look on her face nearly broke my heart. She had heard it too. She also knew what it meant. With tears in her eyes she raced away up the stairs to her room, her heavy school shoes banging on each uncarpeted step. I watched her go. I knew I would have to talk to her later.

I pushed open the living room door, an icy gripping feeling in my gut. A large cloud of blue-grey smoke gusted out the second the door was open. Over the last few months mum had actually taken to smoking out in the garden. The house hadn't been full of fumes, nor did our hair and clothes stink of fag smoke. It had been like living in a new house.

I coughed as I took a lungful of the air. The TV was blaring away. Some stupid antiques show on. Why would my mum be interested in antiques? I guessed it was on while she waited for another of her 'shows' to come on. Catchy theme tune, a glitzy host, and odd contestants. They were her favourites.

'Mum,' I said quietly, trying not to make her jump.

The sound of humming continued. I couldn't see mum, as her chair was positioned with its back to the door, so all I could see was the twirl of cigarette smoke, and one hand that rose above the back of the armchair. It twisted, like the head of a charmed snake, before disappearing again. This was, I assumed, Mum's idea of a wave.

I moved slowly around the room to get a look at Mum. I could already feel tears starting to well up. I had been here before.

I knew Mum was drinking again.

I just didn't know why.

My mum was sprawled on the armchair, humming away to herself. I called out to her again, this time a little louder. On the coffee table was an ashtray, almost full, with a cigarette burning away to nothing lying across one side. A green cheap lighter. The TV remote. A bottle of cheap vodka, three-quarters empty. No glass.

'Mum, what's happened?'

I knew something must have thrown her over the edge. Yesterday she was the mum who helped me with my homework. Today she was this humming, glassy-eyed stranger, sprawled across the chair.

It took me an age to get any sense out of her. I stubbed out the cigarette and sat on the edge of the sofa, holding on to her hand as she hummed and slurred to me. Eventually I went and made her a cup of tea and sneakily slid the bottle of vodka behind my back to stop her drinking any more. I poured it down the sink while I waited for the kettle to boil.

When I brought the tea in I tried again.

'What happened, Mum?'

She looked up at me, her face all screwed up for a moment as if she didn't know who I was, then her face cleared.

'He sacked me.' Her words were joined up and almost not understandable.

'Who did?'

'That bastard at the pub. Jim. Jim the bastard.'

I knew that Jim was the landlord at the pub where Mum had been doing some cleaning for pin money. She had spoken about him a lot and he sounded like an alright bloke.

'Why? What happened?'

'Because. Where's Ivy?'

'She's upstairs in her bedroom, why?'

'Because I don't want her to hear this. He sacked me because I told him I didn't want to give him a blowjob in the cellar any more. He smells weird.'

I don't know why my mum thought I was any better equipped to hear what she said than Ivy was. I may have been a bit older, but this was not a nice thing for anyone to hear from their mum.

'You know what a blowjob is, right?' she slurred at me.

I nodded.

Of course, I knew what it was. I was a thirteen-year-old girl in a mixed comprehensive school. Who had and hadn't given or received a blowjob was a popular a topic of conversation. Almost as popular as what happened on TV last night.

'So, he sacked me. Told me I was a crap cleaner anyway and he only kept me on for the … you know.'

I nodded again.

'I told him to shove it.' She started giggling then, although I couldn't understand why. 'So, I came home and bought myself a little bottle of something with what I got from him.' She beckoned me a little closer, adding, 'I robbed the till as I was on my way out.'

The stench of booze washed over me as she spoke.

'I figured it was the least he owed me. And he can hardly complain, or I'll forget to keep my mouth shut and tell his wife.' She nodded to herself, closing her eyes, and leaning back on the cushions.

I just looked at her. I realised once again how *old* she was looking, especially with the light from the window illuminating her face. Just lately, I thought she had started to look a bit better. After some months of not drinking, her eyes hadn't been so heavy and bloodshot and the little veins in her cheeks had faded away over the summer. But a bottle of vodka seemed to have undone all that.

I realised she had either passed out or fallen asleep. Her steady, sometimes slobbery breathing filled the room.

I went upstairs to drop off my stuff from school and brought a blanket down from Mum's room. I lay it across her. She muttered a little then pulled the blanket up underneath her chin. She seemed comfortable.

I got some tea ready for Ivy and me. While we had tea, Ivy was quiet, pensive. She didn't seem to want to look at Mum at all while she ate. She sat on the floor with her legs crossed, her back to Mum, concentrating on what was on the TV. Once she'd finished her tea, she disappeared back off upstairs to her room and that was the last I saw of her that evening.

I stayed with my mum. She was breathing steadily, and she hadn't thrown up, so that was a bonus. I sat in the same room and did my homework, just turning to check on her now and then.

By about 8pm. I'd finished. I pushed my books back into my bag and ran upstairs to put it away.

When I got back downstairs I walked into the living room. Mum was up, rubbing her face between her hands, and swaying very slightly.

'You OK, Mum?' I said quietly as I came to sit on the arm of her chair. 'I sat down here with you to make sure you were okay. Do you want a cup of tea or something?'

'I want my vodka. That's what I want.'

She sounded angry. So, I slid away from her a bit in case she lashed out. I tried to think what I could say about the vodka.

'I took the empty bottle out in the kitchen, Mum. You'd drank it all.' Thank God it had only been a half bottle, or she might not have woken up at all.

'Liar.' She said it quietly, but I could tell, just from her tone of voice that she was angry.

'Honest, you did. It was empty when I got home.'

She whirled round to face me, having to take a step back to steady herself. This time she yelled.

'You're a lying little fucker.' I knew what was coming and flinched. But despite having her hand raised and ready to dole out a slap, she stopped.

I don't know whether it was me flinching that brought her back from the edge, or just the look of fear on my face, but something made her hold back. Maybe it was some last vestige of sense showing itself, from all the months she had been sober.

She dropped her hand and started to look around the room. She grabbed her fags and the lighter from the table and stomped out of the room, shouting, 'I'm going out.'

The next thing I heard was the front door, crashing closed behind her.

Chapter 8

I went to bed, dreading what sort of state my mum was going to be in when I woke up in the morning.

I awoke at about 1am when the sound of the front door slamming woke me up with a jolt. I threw back the covers of my bed, got up, and poked my head around my door. I thought about going to see if she was okay. But am I glad I didn't.

I stood by my door and listened to what was going on. I couldn't hear properly but I could make out the sound of clinking glasses from downstairs, a raised male voice and the sound of my mum shushing him. The shush carried almost as loudly as his voice.

Satisfied that she was, at least, home and safe, I was happy. But there was no way I was going out to talk to her. I crawled back under my warm covers and tried to go back to sleep, not wishing to be awake to hear the inevitable animal grunts and groans that were sure to follow.

When I woke up again it was gone eight in the morning. I needed the toilet and a drink, so I wrapped myself up in a dressing gown and my slippers. It was already warming up, but there was no way I was going to wander around in just my pyjamas just in case there was still a strange bloke in the house.

I dashed across the landing, trying to be as quiet as possible, and nipped into the toilet. When I'd finished, I came out and stopped at Mum's door before I went downstairs. Although I didn't particularly want to see her, I wanted to know that my mum was okay. I pushed the bedroom door open and slowly poked my head around.

What I actually saw was a bit of shock. Whoever had come home with my mum was fast asleep, face down on the bed. The covers were only half-covering him and his hairy bare backside was showing. I quickly pulled my head back and pulled the door closed. I didn't want Ivy wandering in and getting an eyeful of his bare arse.

I wandered down the stairs and into the living room. It stank, and the place looked like somebody had let off a takeaway bomb. There were tinfoil containers of half-eaten Chinese food littered across the coffee table, on the arms of the sofa, and on the sofa itself. An ashtray was overflowing with butts. And one of my mum's bras was hanging over the back of the sofa.

This was bad. Even when my mum was drinking she kept the place tidy. Ivy and I would get yelled at or worse if we left stuff lying around.

I cleared up the mess. Throwing away food when I was hungry was difficult, so I tried a little bit of the leftover food first. But cold sweet and sour pork was not the best. I spat it out into the bin with the rest of the debris from Mum's night out.

Once I'd tidied up, I made tea and toast and sat on the sofa trying to find something to watch on the TV. We didn't have Sky TV or anything so the channels we did have didn't provide masses of choice. Saturday morning normally meant cartoons.

As I sat drinking my tea, I kept seeing my mum's bra out of the corner of my eye. I picked it up between two fingers and dropped it over the back of the sofa and onto the floor behind. At least it was out of sight now.

I don't really know exactly how much time passed before I heard footsteps coming down the stairs. I knew it wasn't Ivy, the steps were too heavy. It didn't sound like my mum either, as the steps were clear and moving relatively quickly.

I squeezed myself down onto the sofa as much as I could. I'd already seen a strange bloke's backside that morning. If he was wandering around stark bollock naked I really didn't want an eyeful of his crown jewels. The front door slamming came as a blessed relief and I sat back up to watch TV, happy in the knowledge that our little family was now alone.

As I sat there alone, the bright morning sunshine glaring in through the window, picking out every little bit of dust as the particles floated in the sullied air, I couldn't help but wonder what mum was going to be like when she woke up.

I'd got used to her being the nice, normal mum that we'd had for the last few months, and the thought that she was going to fall back into her old ways was scary. There was really no talking to her when had been drinking, so there was little chance of me persuading her to get back on the wagon. But, I knew that for her sake, and for mine and Ivy's, I would have to try.

Chapter 9

Mum got up around midday. You'll never know just how glad I was when I heard her come downstairs that Saturday morning, just before twelve.

The fact that it was *still morning*, even though it was nearly noon, meant two things. First, it meant she had not been *that* drunk the night before (sometimes in the past, she had barely got out of bed at all). Secondly, it meant she wasn't angry with me or Ivy for waking her up.

I hoped and prayed the old habits weren't going to kick straight back in, after so many months of what had felt like normality.

I say 'praying'… I didn't and still don't believe in God. This isn't a story where redemption comes after some kind of epiphany.

I have battled for a long time between whether to blame my mother entirely, partly, or absolve her completely on the grounds of some kind of addictive personality. Ivy and I were let down, there is no doubt in my mind, by my mother. At times she proved that she could be a good mother. But she was also weak. I also think she was probably lonely, resorting to bringing the wrong people into her life to fulfil her need for companionship. So yes, I blame her. But as I've grown older, I've found it in my heart to forgive her.

I didn't need a God to help me do that.

Anyway, after the Friday night blip, that weekend was one of the best I ever remember with my mum. I think she must have been feeling guilty. After sending me off to the shop with money to buy bacon, she made lunch for everyone – bacon sandwiches!

I remember sitting on the sofa, stomach growling, waiting while she cooked. I could hear the spit, spatter, and sizzle of the bacon cooking, my mum swearing to herself when a particularly vicious spit of fat must have landed on her bare hand. I didn't like that much. My mum normally only swore when she had been drinking. Then she put her head around the door with a half-grimace, half-smile on her face.

'Sorry, kids. Bloody fat spat on my hand.'

Two nervous kids turned toward her and smiled back. She never said sorry normally when she had been drinking.

It felt to me that we were teetering on the edge of a dangerous chasm. On one side was safe ground (no alcohol, and a mum that made bacon sandwiches). On the side was a mum that drank, and with it, a deep ravine of fear and hopelessness. That small apology had felt like a step towards safe ground.

When the sandwiches arrived, the delicious taste of salty bacon in bread, crisp and greasy, was like manna from heaven, and another leap to safety

The rest of that day I was on edge. I so hoped the Friday night was a momentary blip, a slip off the wagon, but with an immediate remount.

As it turned out, we had a good day. All three of us sat on the sofa. I was the only one dressed after running to the shop. Mum and Ivy stayed in dressing gowns and PJs. We watched TV. We drank tea. Mum helped Ivy with some homework then washed up the lunch dishes.

The biggest surprise came at about 6pm.

My mum did something really unexpected.

She found her purse and pulled out a crisp new £20 note and handed it to me. I was awestruck. It sounds ridiculous, but I'd never seen that much money before in my life.

'Go round the chippy and get us all some tea, love,' she said.

I just sat there on the sofa looking at the note in my hand.

'Amy?' she said, 'Are you alright?'

I looked up at her. I must have looked like a bit of a loon. I just stared at her with my mouth open.

'Are you sure, Mum?' I said, 'What about the bills?'

'Don't you worry about that,' she said, 'there's more where that came from.'

I could see another two twenties in her purse.

'Where d'you get all that money, Mum?' I asked, astounded to see so much in there. Normally it was no more than a couple of fivers and a few coins.

'From Ray.' She leaned in a bit further to me and whispered in my ear, 'I sold some stuff for Ray.'

'Who's Ray? What stuff?'

'I met him in the pub. He came back last night.'

I was able to put a name to the backside I'd seen that morning. That was more than normally happened. Generally, Mum's visitors dodged out the next morning without saying a word. If Mum ever remembered their names, she never bothered telling us.

'What did you sell for him?'

'Never you mind, it was just some stuff he wanted to get rid of. So, I helped him out and he paid me.'

I wasn't a complete innocent. I had heard talk from most of the kids about drugs, and when somebody talked about selling stuff, it was either drugs or stolen goods. None of that was good. The only other selling I knew about were those women who sold themselves. A quick shag or a blowjob for twenty quid in the alleys that ran behind the streets we lived in. I didn't think Mum would have done that. Of course, Ray might have paid her for the night he spent with her, but that didn't seem like Mum. I was sure she was either flogging drugs for him or stolen goods. I looked at her, not knowing how to react. Mum just ignored my reaction, put away her purse and carried on watching TV.

'I'll have cod and chips, love,' she said, her eyes glued to some game show.

In the end I had a choice. A full belly of fish and chips, which we hadn't had since coming back from Nan's in the summer, or nothing to eat, a stroppy mother, and probably a slap for good measure.

I went and fetched my coat.

When I got back there were three plates waiting on the worktop in the kitchen, and three slices of buttered bread. The glorious smell of fried fish and chips soon filled the house. It was mixed with the sharp tang of vinegar that the guy in the chippy would sprinkle on without asking.

Good job we all liked our vinegar with our chips!

The food was awesome. Crisp batter and juicy white fish. Golden chips. Best of all was the chip butties we made with the slice of bread. Our fingers got covered in the butter and grease that dripped out of the bottom of the sandwich whenever we took a bite.

I looked over at Ivy who was speed-eating for England, hoovering up her food like she would never be fed again. I couldn't blame her. There had been enough times in the past where bread and jam made up all three meals in a day.

I slid a few of my chips onto her plate. She looked up from her food just long enough to smile and say thank you before she was head down again.

By the time we finished, none of us could move. We were so stuffed, our bellies bulging with the amount of food we had all eaten. Good job I hadn't bought banana fritters for afters!

The rest of that evening was magical. We sat on the sofa and talked as if we were three girls on a sleepover. I had to guess what that was like because I had never been on one, but I was willing to bet it was like that night.

We drank tea. We watched TV. We talked. We were like what I thought a normal family was like - one of those families in the posh houses.

By the time 10pm came around I was ready to sleep. Doing nothing all day wears me out more than working and I was ready for my bed. Mum turned off the TV. She hadn't had a drink all day.

That day had proved again that she wasn't always a bad mother. We were warm, had full stomachs and she had spent some time with us.

Chapter 10

The whole weekend was awesome. The Saturday was good, after a shaky start, but the Sunday was an absolute dream.

Now what I'm about to say might all sound a bit lowbrow and boring for a lot of people who might be reading this. But for me and Ivy, what we did that Sunday was so unusual that it seemed mind-blowing at the time.

We went to a car boot sale.

Now I know a lot of people who love a car boot. I still like them now. I also know that there are a lot of people who wouldn't be seen dead buying anything at a car boot sale. But this was the first one I'd ever been to. Uncle Tony came over in his car to pick all three of us up and take us there. It was great to see him again and lovely to be out in the countryside.

After we parked up I took a look around. The place was absolutely heaving with people. Everybody seemed to have bought their dog with them. Ivy was in seventh heaven, she loves dogs and spent most of her time fussing them as we passed. In the end Uncle Tony had to hold her hand and pull her along otherwise we'd have got absolutely nowhere.

I loved the place. There was a sense of excitement in the air. Most of the stands were full of junk. But on every stand, I always found something that interested me. I guess I must have been a bit of a magpie because it was usually something small and shiny that caught my eye.

But sometimes, it was a book that attracted me. I could have gone away from there with enough books to have filled an entire library but instead I persuaded Uncle Tony to buy me three dog-eared Harry Potter books.

I was so excited. I knew there was no chance of ever buying copies of Harry Potter for myself. I did try at the library, but they were always out on loan. So, as with many other things, I had gone without.

A cheerfully fat woman (who was probably not so fat without the big woolly hat and scarf and multiple layers of clothes she was wearing) said that I could have *all three* for the £1 coin my Uncle Tony handed over. It felt like nothing short of a miracle.

I've always loved reading. The words seem to paint pictures in my mind. And as it turned out, those three Harry Potter books were more than just entertainment over the next few months. They took me away to a place of magic and wonder when my reality was to become place of darkness and fear.

The books were all I bought at the car boot. Oh, and a great big burger from one of the catering vans. That was awesome too.

You might notice a bit of a theme running through my story – I was always happy when my belly was full. Bear in mind, I never knew for sure when I was going to get another proper meal. That love of food has followed me through into my adult life. I still have to watch out that I don't just binge eat to keep me feeling happy.

That Sunday afternoon we went back to Uncle Tony's place. Auntie Jo had stayed behind with Jason and indulged in her hobby which, lucky for me and Ivy, was baking.

Homemade bread and cakes were something else neither of us had ever experienced before. It seemed such a luxury.

But I started to feel a little guilty that we might be making mum feel bad. She must have noticed the difference between Tony and Jo's modern, clean, and tidy house and their dining room table groaning under the weight of more food than I ever set eyes on. Often, our dinner at home was beans or spaghetti out of a tin on toast.

I could sense my mum was acting a bit quiet. I wanted to tell her, whatever happened, she was still my mum, whether she made cupcakes or not. But instead I just watched as she smoked in the back garden, not talking to anyone.

She always seemed resentful of what other people had without realising that she could have it too if she only got off her backside and worked for it. I don't think she ever thought, 'I'm going to sort myself out and try to get something similar'.

Much as I would like to think that we can all change our situation, I also know that for some people, life is tougher than it is for others. Mental health issues, self-worth issues, they all work to stop some people ever finding find their own way out of their problems. But right then, eating the topping off a homemade cupcake, watching as my mum smoked and sulked in my uncle's back garden, I wished she would do something to help herself.

Little did I know that she *did* have plans for the future, but the route she took wasn't via college to finish her education or starting a little business. Her way forward was to turn my life into a living hell.

***

When I got back from school on Monday, the rot had already set in. It had been an ordinary day at school. On my way home, I'd met up with Ivy and we decided to make the most of the decent weather by going to the park on the way home. We stayed for half an hour, then slowly made our way home, wondering if mum had cooked or not. When we got home, the signs were all good. I could smell cooking in the air, although I could also smell fag smoke as usual.

We both shouted our hellos and rushed upstairs to dump our bags and change out of our school clothes. (We both used to do that every day to try and stop them smelling of fags.)

We both then ran downstairs to eat.

I can remember this moment as if it happened yesterday. We both went into the living room, me first with Ivy close behind. I stopped suddenly, and she ran into my back. Sitting on our sofa was a man, tucking in to fried eggs on toast.

'Right then, you two,' Mum said. 'This is Ray, and where the hell have you been until this time?'

Chapter 11

That night, I lay in my bed hearing the usual noises from my mum's room next door. Even with my pillow clamped so tight around my head that I could barely breathe, I could still hear the animal sounds.

I knew only too well what they were doing, and mostly I didn't mind. I understood that Mum had needs, even if it did gross me out. If she chose to fulfil them, then that was her business and I had no right to tell her not to. And, if this new bloke was anything like the others, it wouldn't be long before he'd bugger off, never to be seen again.

Most weeks it was only ever a Friday or Saturday night that Mum brought blokes back to the house. Mum's weekend activities didn't affect me. It didn't matter if I was kept awake by her and her men friends when there was no school the next day. But this was a Monday and I had to get up in the morning for school. Mum and Ray had been up drinking, shouting and talking until really late before they went to bed. I got almost no sleep at all that night.

The next morning, I was late getting up and although breakfast was only ever toast, I had to skip it to make sure I got to school on time. I was so tired I felt like I was trying to swim through treacle all day. It was all I could do to stay awake.

When I came home that afternoon, Ray was still there. I ate my tea, then sat uncomfortably in front of the TV while Mum and Ray sat on the sofa, drinking beer and smoking. Ivy disappeared off to her room early, and just after nine I went too.

When I got up in the morning, I went downstairs to find the living room looking like somebody had come in and emptied a bin bag around the place. The plates from dinner were still lying around, and there were more beer cans than I'd ever seen before. Some of them had tipped up and spilled their contents on the floor. The two ashtrays were full to overflowing and the place generally looked like a complete tip.

Now, mum was never the tidiest or cleanest mum ever, she was certainly no clean freak. But she did always keep the place reasonably tidy. I had honestly never seen the place looking so disgusting.

I didn't know it at the time, but this state of affairs was going to become the norm. And my life was about to change from being a happy, if slightly deprived kid, to... well I can't really describe what I was turned into by the events that were about to happen.

When I got home from school, someone had made a bit of an effort to clean up, but the place still looked pretty bad. The room reeked of mum's cigarettes. Ray smoked roll ups which smelled a bit better than mum's, but the room was full of smoke.

Now, I am not some rabid anti-smoker. I don't smoke myself as an adult, but I wouldn't deny anyone who wanted to smoke. But when they both lit up at the same time, I just hated it. The room would quickly fill with blue-grey smoke that would float, almost in layers in the air. Half the time I couldn't make out the TV because my eyes would water, and I'd start to cough to try and clear the tickle in my throat.

One thing I always liked was staying over at my friends' houses, or having them stay over with me. I had two main friends, Sarah and Jay. I would go around to theirs and they would come around to mine. I always enjoyed having my friends around. I had no idea really at the time of the kind of deprivation Ivy and I were living in because my friends were in a similar situation. None of us gave a bit of notice to how the others lived. It was just friendship.

The two girls were a bit like me in many ways. None of us were part of what were called the 'popular' girls. We three were part of the great central mass of kids who didn't belong to any particular group, trying to find our own way in life, muddling through as best we could whatever our individual circumstances.

They would come around and we would do the normal kind of stuff that teenage girls do. We would laugh and giggle about inane things, talk about boys, gossip, listen to music, and dream about where we wanted to end up. And yes, we talked about what kind of dream man might be interested in us.

Once Ray came on the scene, that pretty much came to an end. We went from living in a poor but tidy house, to surviving in a pigsty whenever he was around. And he was now staying around several times a week, and all weekend. I just couldn't invite my friends around when he was there. I didn't want them to see how bad the house had got since he arrived on the scene. It was the first time I ever remember feeling ashamed of my mum and the way we lived.

I couldn't see what she saw in Ray. He wasn't particularly good-looking and some of his teeth were missing. He had scratchy tattoos on his neck, and always had stubble on his chin. He was tall, I'll admit, but really thin and bony. He wasn't particularly interesting or fun either. He just watched TV, got drunk, ate and smoked. He would laugh at the TV, but not much at anything else. He also gave me the creeps. He was around at ours all the time, but never made any effort to get to know me or Ivy. He barely spoke to us most of the time. I always felt uncomfortable when he was around, like I couldn't properly relax. I'd had barely anything to do with the bloke since he had been coming around, preferring to stay in my room and read. I don't think we'd said more than ten words to each other at this point. I was secretly hoping Mum would dump him so we could get back to normal. But then, Mum dropped a bombshell on us none of us was expecting.

'Ray's going to be staying with us for a while,' she said as she stumbled into the living room, one early afternoon Saturday after a night out the day before.

My heart sank.

'Don't start moaning if you find him in the bathroom either,' Mum said.

I didn't know at the time, but Ray's arrival on the scene was a turning point. We, as a whole family were about to be taken down, almost as far as anyone can be taken down.

Chapter 12

Life with Ray in the house fell into a kind of weird routine. I would wait until I knew he wasn't in the bathroom in the mornings to go in and take care of what I needed to do. In the evenings, I'd watch TV for an hour with him and Mum, and then Ivy and I would spend the rest of the night upstairs. Sometimes, we spent the evenings just sitting reading or messing about in each other's rooms.

When we were at school I always felt a huge sense of release that I could go about my life without having to think about Ray and whatever he and Mum were up to.

School was finally starting to come good. I wasn't great with every subject. But certainly, in Maths and English, I had got myself toward the top of the class. This was down to all the extra work I was doing and, of course, with the help of my teachers who were by and large supportive. There were still one or two diehards who didn't think anyone from the area I lived in could ever do well at school. In fact, I'm convinced, even to this day, that there were one or two who were prejudiced against kids like me. Some didn't think we deserved to do well, no matter how much effort we put in.

My after-school routine had changed as soon as Ray started living with us. I tried to find an excuse to stay out as long as I could. And after whatever paltry dinner my mum had got ready, I would escape up to my room. Away from the grim reality of crap lying around and the smoky smell, I'd read Harry Potter and retreat into a world of wizardry and magic.

At weekends I had no way of escaping. I use to pray to the weather gods that it was nice outside so at least I would be able to get out and play. It sounds a bit childish that at thirteen I was still going out to 'play'. That's just what we called spending time outside.

Lots of the small kids in our estate seemed to be attracted to me like magnets. And I'd often spent the whole day playing, what seemed to me to be, stupid kid games. Skipping rope games, clambering across the monkey bars and all that kind of thing. Despite everything, I always knew I wanted to be a mother one day.

So, at weekends, wherever possible, I was outside in the almost-fresh air. I would happily spend all day out there even though we lived close to a dual-carriageway and there was always a faint smell of diesel fumes around.

Saturdays in particular, I would do my level best to stay outside until about 6. If I could manage that, by the time I got home, Mum and Ray would be getting ready to go down the pub for their weekly blowout.

I knew where all the money was coming from to pay for all the beer and cigarettes. Where else would they get that sort of money? They had both been on benefits until someone reported that Ray was living with us. When they both ended up getting their benefits cut, it caused a couple of days of hellish arguments in the house. But strangely, neither of them seemed to be any worse off than they were before.

The pair of them were dealing weed to fund their lifestyle. That was obvious. We didn't have hundreds of plants growing under bright lights in the loft, or outside in the backyard, and we never had a constant stream of people traipsing to the front door. I think they must have been dealing in the pub.

Whatever they were doing, they were getting enough money so they could keep themselves in beer and fags, and spare enough to just about feed me and Ivy. But it was never enough to do anything to improve our lifestyle. No half-term trips to the cinema, or weekends away like the posh kids got.

Holidays like half-term were a bit of nightmare. If the weather was dry, we would be good. We would be out and about and keeping out of the way. If it was bad we could try to use the shed to stay out of the house but sometimes, if it was really cold and wet out, we had no choice but to stay in the house. I hated those days.

Mum and Ray spent every day drinking and smoking. In the evening, they took to smoking weed, when they would drink some more. My mum was starting to look even older than she had before, and Ray was turning creepy. On the odd occasion when we did all eat together, I would look up and catch him looking at me weirdly. He would leer at me, then lick his lips, showing off the gaps in his teeth. When I caught him at it he would just stare at me, then turn away with a smile on his face.

I tried to tell my mum that Ray was looking at me funny, but she laughed at me and told me I was just imagining things. Ray was her bloke so why would he be looking at me? I couldn't answer that. I didn't know why he was looking at me, just when he did, it made me feel incredibly uncomfortable.

So that was how our lives were progressing. I was doing my best to keep up at school, while almost every day, my mum and Ray got pissed and stoned.

I'd noticed Ivy looking at Ray from time to time with a really upset look on her face, especially when he treated her like a little kid or took the mickey out of her for being small. He called her a 'titch' and pretended to swat her, like a fly. When she spoke, he'd say, 'Did you hear something? Was that a mouse squeaking?'

I was strong enough to put up with the jibes and ignore them, but Ivy? I wasn't so sure. She was only small and not very confident. Whenever Ray started on us, my mum either did nothing, was too pissed to notice, or simply joined in with the joke.

Chapter 13

Ray had been living with us for about a month when I had first caught him looking at me. Another few months down the road and he was still at it. And it was starting to get on my nerves. I even asked him to stop. But he said he was 'only looking', and that he didn't mean anything by it. In the end, I decided the best thing I could do was just to ignore him, and keep out of his and Mum's way as much as possible.

That is what I did.

It was a wet, cold day in November when the real trouble began with Ray. There was something on the TV I really wanted to watch – Harry Potter and the Philosopher's Stone. It was the first of the films and I was desperate to watch it. So desperate that I actually encouraged Mum and Ray to get pissed and get stoned. When they were stoned, they would just sit there quiet, hardly saying anything.

I even smiled at Ray when he started talking to me, in the vain hope that he might keep drinking himself into oblivion. Then, I could sit and watch the film in relative peace. I would have loved the option of being able to just sit and watch it in my room like a lot of the other kids. But I knew that would never happen.

Ray went through a couple of stages when he drank, before he finally reached the too-pissed-to-stand-up stage.

After the first couple of cans he would get noisy and boisterous, like a big noisy dog, only constantly delivering verbal abuse to me and Ivy. I had learned to put up with that. I didn't let what he was saying get to me. I even pretended to laugh at him a couple of times, so he didn't let his anger get the better of him.

My least favourite stage came up after three or four cans. That is when he would look at me weirdly. I sometimes encouraged him to have some more weed as that seemed to help him progress to the final stage, which was close to unconsciousness.

This was Ray at his best. Because then I could just ignore him.

'I'll do you a deal, Amy,' he said to me.

'What is it?'

'You try one.'

'What? No. I don't want one.' He was waving his baccy tin in front of my nose. It was where he kept his joints, rolled up and ready to go.

'Go on, you should try one. It makes you relax.' He turned his head to bark at my mum who was by this time already at stage three. 'Doesn't it, love?'

She muttered something incomprehensible where she sat slumped on the sofa next to Ray.

I had tried smoking a few fags in my time. There probably wasn't a kid in the area who hadn't, and I know a lot of the other kids around had experimented with weed before too. But the smell of the weed was so rank that I didn't think I would ever be able to smoke one. It was so *sickly*.

I looked at the tin as the theme music for the film started up. I was desperate to watch it and although I really didn't fancy the idea, I took one of his weed ciggies out of the tin. I was really hoping he would pass out as soon, so I could stub it out and watch my film.

'Mum?' I said, holding out the joint while Ray searched in his trouser pocket, then down the side of the sofa for his lighter. She looked over, her eyes hooded and her head swaying from side to side.

'Mum, Ray wants to me have a joint. What should I do.'

Slowly, she managed to focus her eyes enough to see what I was holding. After a few seconds she just shrugged her shoulders and mumbled something. It sounded like, 'I don't give a fuck,' but she was slurring so much that I couldn't be sure.

Ray had lit his joint and taken a tug on it, then blew the smoke out into the room where it billowed around in front of the TV, the smoke taking on the colours of the screen as the first scenes played in the film. He leaned over and clicked his lighter in front of my face. The flame flicked up.

'I'll just do this to get him to shut the fuck up, so I can watch my film in peace,' I thought.

I'd never really felt much of an urge to experiment with drugs like other kids had. When you live with someone who can barely function because of drugs and booze, the glamourous façade that drugs seem to be given on TV fades away really quick. The first time you have to help your mum to the toilet and clean her up after she's vomited or pissed herself really does take the edge off any desire to try yourself.

But this was different. I had a reason to try it that would suit me. I lit of the joint and took the first pull on it. I immediately got the smell that I found so sickly-sweet inside my mouth as I inhaled, then blew out the smoke.

I didn't feel any different … for about thirty seconds … then the room started to spin. The taste in my mouth was horrible and I could feel my stomach rolling as my brain and body rebelled against the drug.

I dropped the still smoking joint into the ashtray and, feeling like I was going to hurl up, ran for the bathroom. I spent the next half hour, sitting on the cold bathroom floor, heaving but not puking much, mopping my brow with toilet paper, not daring to move until the heaves had stopped, just in case I couldn't get back to the toilet in time.

I then crawled to my bedroom and managed to clamber into my bed. The room was still spinning, and I prayed I wouldn't puke up in my sleep. Eventually I must have drifted off.

I woke up with a start. My head felt like thunderclouds were rolling around inside. I had a pounding headache, my brain felt fuzzy and I had a raging thirst. I stumbled down the stairs and into the kitchen where I got a large glass of water.

Next, I did two really stupid things. Stupid thing number one was to go back into the living room. Ray and my mum were both well-gone by that point. Ray had his head in my mum's lap fast asleep and snoring, my mum was just staring blankly ahead of her, not even noticing as I came in.

Stupid thing number two was picking up the joint out of the ashtray and lighting it up with Ray's lighter.

Don't ask me why I did it. I have no idea why I did, especially after how much I had hated the first drag of weed. It's something I've regretted doing for the longest time. But I've learned to accept that there are times when my logical brain takes a wrong turn and ends up doing something monumentally idiotic. That was such an occasion.

Chapter 14

Things progressed from there. I took to sharing weed with Mum and Ray every night, after Ivy had gone upstairs. It made the evenings go so much easier. I came to quite enjoy sitting there with the two of them, even though once I had hated it.

Things came to a full head a few weeks later. It was one particular night when I'd had some weed. I was sitting downstairs with Mum and Ray. Ray popped a tin of beer and, instead of drinking it, he passed it over to me. I looked at Mum, who didn't bat an eyelid. So, I drank the beer. I liked the way the bitter flavour of it took away the taste of the weed.

Ray was at stage two. It was his flirting and innuendo stage. A days earlier he had teased me about not having a boyfriend. I'd laughed along with him, but I was still embarrassed. I'd never even kissed a boy and although I wasn't completely clueless about sex, I'd not even had a fumble behind the bike sheds.

That night the sexual conversation got more serious. He started to ask me if I'd let a boyfriend finger me? I had no idea what to say. My mum was absolutely no use whatsoever. She was mumbling and muttering in her normal spot surrounded by fag ends and empty beer cans.

If I had a boyfriend, would I let him fuck me? Would I suck his cock?

I shook my head. I couldn't think of what to say to him. In a very strange way, it almost made me feel grown up, talking about that sort of thing with an adult. Now I've had time to look into the subject, it is clear that it was nothing more than his way of grooming me. But at the time, a time when I was growing and developing from a young girl into a woman, it actually made me feel somehow special. And, the combination of beer and weed and a healthy dose of embarrassment meant it also seemed quite funny.

So, I laughed.

He laughed too.

I laughed so much that, after three cans of beer, I was desperate for a pee. I dashed off up the stairs still laughing about what had happened.

When I came out of the toilet Ray was there. In front of me. He was big, at least a foot taller me than me and although he was skinny he was muscly. Wiry. I backed up straight into the bathroom and he followed me in.

'You been for a piss?' I could smell him as he got closer. It's a difficult smell to describe, a mixture of fags, booze, weed, and body odour. It's like nothing I'd ever smelt before and a smell I will always remember as long as I live.

I nodded my head at his question. He put his hand on my shoulder, either to hold me up or himself, I'm still not sure.

'Let me check if you wiped yourself proper.'

I couldn't move. He was holding me, but my drunken brain wouldn't seem to let me *do* anything to stop this ugly beast from touching me. With one quick move, he had put his hand down inside my pyjama bottoms, between my legs, and pushed a finger into me.

It was over in a flash, or so it seemed.

That was the first time.

I should have known that he would try again. And try again he did. Lots of times. And always when I had been on the weed or had a can of beer.

Why didn't I stop smoking and drinking with him? I really don't know the answer to that question and I dare say that there will be a few people that would say it was my own fault. But I was little more than a kid. I was conflicted immensely. The attention fed my ego, and I thought it did me good. But every time he touched me, I wanted to hurl on him.

In the end something was going to have to crack and it turned out to be me. After he'd finished touching me one day I told him. 'I'm going to tell Mum if you keep on doing that to me. You shouldn't be doing it. I'm only thirteen.'

'Tell her if you like. She don't care. You've seen what she's like. Five minutes after you tell her she'll have forgotten.'

He sneered at me then, coming closer and holding me be the jaw. I was so scared that I didn't even react when he put his hand up my top. At age thirteen, there was nothing there for him to grab.

'You tell her. See what she says.'

He let me go and I managed to dodge round him and slip into my bedroom. I sat in my room and prayed for the night to pass so I could talk to Mum in the morning. I'd make sure she knew all about the pig who was ruining our lives. I'd make sure she got him out of the house.

Chapter 15

Nothing happened.

It was a few days after I had threatened Ray and he hadn't touched me since. But I was determined to say something. If I told Mum what he had done, she would see what sort of bloke he was and kick him out. Then life could go back to being good again. I was standing in front of my Mum while she was doing something in the kitchen.

'Mum.'

'What?' She was searching through the fridge, probably for something for us all to eat.

'Ray keeps touching me.'

'What do you mean?'

'He gets me in the bathroom and touches me. He puts his hand down my pants and ... you know.'

She didn't turn around, but she stopped rattling around in the fridge. I heard her sigh then she span around to face me. I took a step back. Her face was full of anger.

'What are you telling me that for?'

'Because it's not right, Mum. I want you to tell him to stop.'

'It's only Ray, Amy.'

'What? I know who it is, Mum.'

'Well it's not such a big deal is it? It's only a bit of fiddling around.'

'What? Mum?'

I couldn't believe what I was hearing. What Ray had said was true, she really didn't care. And right now, she wasn't even pissed.

'Don't you ruin this for me, Amy.'

And that was it, she grabbed a small lump of cheese out of the fridge and disappeared back into the living room.

I was dumbfounded. She was the one person on the whole world who could stop this. The one person I should have been able to rely on. And all she was bothered about was not losing her boyfriend, despite what he was doing to me.

I turned around to go upstairs and cry. It's all I wanted to do right at that moment. But leaning in the doorway was Ray. He had his arms crossed and broad grin on his face. He had heard the whole conversation. He took a step forward as I took a step back, then he pushed the door to the living room closed.

I kept going backwards as far as I could until my back bumped up against the fridge. I could feel my heart beating like crazy in my chest. I held my school bag up in front of me with both hands. I was terrified and shaking. What Mum had said now gave him free rein.

He shoved one hand against my bag, forcing me roughly against the fridge. Then, holding me with one hand, put the other hand up my school skirt and into my knickers.

He looked down at me and grinned with his ugly gappy mouth. He was so close I could smell his grim breath wafting over my face. He took his hand away but still held me back against the fridge.

'Told you,' he said. Then he turned away, opened the door to the living room and disappeared inside.

I ran, straight upstairs, slamming my door behind me. I sat on my bed and cried, the horrible feeling of the touch of his hand on me, burning into my skin.

I was so miserable sitting there, crying my heart out, tears dripping off my nose onto my third-hand school tie, that I couldn't imagine that things could get any worse. Short of stabbing Ray in the middle of the night (something I had seriously considered), I couldn't see a way out.

At school the subject of child abuse had been covered briefly and the advice always was to tell somebody. But who could I tell? I'd already told my mum and she wasn't going to do anything about it. I could tell a teacher at school but that would be *so* shameful, especially now that I was doing so well. Plus, the social would be down on us like a ton of bricks. I didn't want to end up in care and I didn't want to be split up from Ivy.

Perhaps I could tell Uncle Tony. But he was my mum's brother. He was a man, too. Would he even be bothered? Perhaps I could tell Auntie Jo? I just wasn't sure what to do. I didn't have many choices, as I saw it.

But whatever I did, I should have acted sooner. I should have told someone, anyone.

Because before long, events began to spiral even further out of control.

It was only a few days later when he touched me again. I screamed at him to take his filthy mitts off me at the top of my voice. He just laughed. Right in my face. His breath made me want to puke, it was so disgusting. I ran down the stairs and stood in front of my mum, so she couldn't just ignore me and watch the telly. I screamed in her face, telling her what he had done, asking her, telling her she needed to do something about him.

She wasn't too pissed at the time as it was still early evening, so she looked at me with her eyes focused clearly on me.

'For fuck's sake, Amy. He's only fingering you a bit. All blokes do it. I swear, Amy, if he leaves because of you, I'll swing for you. Now fuck off out my way, my show's starting in a minute.'

Chapter 16

The inevitable happened one evening. I was downstairs. I'd had a beer, but since the time in the kitchen I had sworn off the weed. So, I was feeling quite level-headed. I'd had a good day at school although Mr Jacobs asked if I was okay because my test scores were down a bit. I'd been finding it more and more difficult to concentrate, lying awake at night wondering if he would be waiting for me if I went for a pee.

I went out into the kitchen to get myself a cup of tea and I could hear Ray and my mum talking about something. I didn't pay that much attention, I was still really conscious about the kettle and making sure I was careful with it after Ivy's accident. Mum swore that if we ever had to go to A

& E, or 'Casualty', as it was called then, we would probably have the social down on us like a ton of bricks, and I really didn't want that to happen.

The kettle was rumbling away, coming to the boil as I dropped a teabag into the cup. The TV was blaring in the living room. Although I could hear Ray's deep voice, I couldn't hear what he was saying. His voice didn't sound angry or anything, so I wasn't that bothered. I was going to make my tea then go upstairs to read before I went to sleep. Hopefully.

As I passed the living room, through the door I heard Ray say, 'So can I?'

My mum replied, 'I don't care, do what you like.' She had that bored sound to her voice again, like she was hardly even listening.

I didn't think too much of it. I said goodnight and headed off upstairs. I'd just finished my cup of tea, and was in my PJs, sitting up in bed reading when I heard a squeak of a stair. I didn't think much of it at first, but then I put down my book and looked at my door.

The handle started to turn. I could feel a sharp stab of fear run down my spine. I knew it wasn't Ivy. Her bedroom door made a sound when she opened it and besides, she usually just burst into my room.

Ray stepped through the door. He closed it behind himself then just stood there.

'What do you want?' I said. I was petrified, unable to move. I had pulled my knees up when he came in and all I could think of doing was trying to curl up so tight that I disappeared into myself. If I made myself as tiny as possible, maybe he would go away.

'You know what I want,' he said. He was right. I think I'd known this moment was coming the first time my mum said she didn't care about what he did to me. For some reason, I had put the thought out of my head. I wish I hadn't. I wish I had acted on my fears earlier. Because he had decided to make his move tonight, a move he had probably been planning for some time.

I wanted to run but he was too strong for me, I knew right then what was going to happen and I had a choice, to fight or to take it. In the end, I fought him, even though I knew I would come off worst from it. But he was twice my weight and freaky strong. I remember him pulling off my PJ bottoms and dropping his pants. I remember trying to imagine myself somewhere magical and far away from what was happening.

I remembered back to our lovely holiday at my nan's that summer. I imagined I was there, in the pitch black, lying down on her back lawn and looking up into the darkness as a perfect blanket of stars twinkled down at me. I imagine being gathered up and carried away until I was just a tiny speck in the sky where I could shine down, and nobody would be able to hurt me anymore.

I remember a lot of pain. But I guess it was probably no more than a few minutes before he had finished. I heard him grunt, then he was standing up.

'You're a good girl, Amy. Don't tell anyone about this. Just between you and me. Okay?' I said nothing. I just wanted him away from me, out of my room, out of what had once been my little sanctuary. This room would never be the same again.

I can't remember too much after that. I think I must have just blanked out the trauma of it. All I can remember after he left was cleaning myself up and trying to go to sleep.

Chapter 17

Over the next few weeks the same thing happened again and again. Each time was the same. I turned fourteen while this was going on, and despite being strong mentally, I couldn't do anything to stop it happening. He knew that whatever he did, I wouldn't say anything. I was too scared of what would happen if the social found out.

My mum had sunk even more into a drunken, weed filled morass, drinking from morning 'til night. Every morning, she started the day with 'a big fat bifter to get me going'. That was her word for a joint.

I like to think she was feeling guilty for what she was letting happen to me but I'm not sure she ever did. I'm not even sure she was fully aware of exactly what was happening. I mean, she knew it was going on, but I think she just pretended she didn't.

After a time, the inevitable happened. I missed my period. When I missed the second one, I had to tell my mum. She took it quite calmly when I told her. But there was a big row that night when I had gone to bed.

I actually didn't mind being pregnant. I didn't want a child, but at the same time, it might be an escape from my situation. Was I selfish to want to use a baby in that way? Yes, maybe. But until you are in that situation, only then would you understand how utterly fucked up your thought processes become.

In the end, I didn't get a choice.

In the days before the doctor's appointment, Ray and my mum must have spent that time concocting a plausible sounding story to explain away a fourteen-year-old girl being pregnant. When we got there, Mum sounded well-prepared. She acted like a normal concerned mother.

'She's always been a bit wild, Doctor Sharman. She's a lot of trouble for us. Just lately, she's been sleeping with this boy and she's got caught out. But my husband, Amy's dad, he had a word with the lad concerned and scared him away.' I turned to her looking puzzled, Ray wasn't my dad. He wasn't even close to being any sort of parent. Mum went on, 'Since we got rid of that lad, everything has been much better at home. Amy has promised to knuckle down after the abortion and we are trying to work together as a family.'

I'm almost certain that the doctor rolled his eyes at me. He'd probably heard it all a million times before. I never spoke the whole time I was there. I just listened when the doctor told me how lucky I was to have a supporting family. Many parents would have chucked me out, he said.

'This is your last chance, Amy,' he said. 'No one is sort things out for you next time. So, you need to buck up your ideas or you'll end up like all those other girls out there.' I just nodded, desperately trying not to cry. Here I was, pregnant by the man who was supposed to be looking after me, fourteen years old, scared to death, and the doctor thought it was all my own fault.

I had the abortion two weeks later, right in the Easter holidays, so I didn't have to miss any time off school. When I came back from the clinic I felt awful, both in my body and in my head.

But something had changed in me. And I was pretty sure I would cut Ray's bollocks off if he came anywhere near me. But he never touched me again. Perhaps the pregnancy scared him off.

Once I was back at school things seemed to calm down a little bit at home. I started doing my extra work again. Despite everything, nothing was going to stop me doing what I wanted to do. The sooner I got the qualifications I needed to get the hell away from the estate, from Ray and sadly from my mother, the better life would be.

I felt so grown up at the time, but I was still having such childish thoughts. You see, I imagined I'd be taking Ivy with me to college, to university, to another town, or wherever I went. How would that work? I hadn't thought it through.

It was about some months after my trip to the clinic when the shit really hit the fan.

'Get off, Ray, you shouldn't be doing that.' The words were followed by a high-pitched scream.

It was Ivy.

Chapter 18

I had shot up the stairs and into Ivy's bedroom. Ray was standing with his back to me, standing over the tiny Ivy. Despite still being still only fourteen, I found the strength to yank this grown man away from my little sister.

I wasn't sure how far things had gone.

I was furious.

So was he.

So was Ivy.

Mum was downstairs in front of the TV. Where else would she be?

I was shaking like a leaf, but I stood there staring him down. I knew the hell I'd been put through by this man, and I was determined, desperate almost, that Ivy wouldn't have to suffer the indignity and pain that I'd been through.

He had gone too far. I didn't care what happened to me, but Ivy was *twelve*. What sort of a sick bastard looks at a twelve-year-old in that way? And what sort of a life would she have if Ray got his hands on her now? It was time to fight back. I just had to get him away from Ivy.

'You lay one finger on her Ray and I promise, I will call the police.'

'You won't. You don't want to go into care.' He knew my darkest fear. But this time, I couldn't let it stop me. I had to face up to whatever was going to happen next, whatever that was, even if it meant going into a children's home, I would cope. The only thing I wasn't going to let happen was him touching Ivy.

'I'd rather go into care than let you touch Ivy! And remember, if we get taken away, you'll be going to jail. They don't like people like you in there do they?' I wasn't sure about this, but I'd heard stories about kiddy-fiddlers in prison, and hoped that they were true.

Ray's face was now angry. I could see in his eyes that he wanted to hurt me. But I wasn't scared. He could overpower me physically if he really wanted. But if he laid one finger on Ivy, they'd find him one morning with a kitchen knife sticking out of his chest. I was really that desperate.

'You wouldn't.'

'I would Ray. And my teacher at school knows there is something up. I haven't said anything but if something was to slip out when I'm upset …'

I left the rest of the phrase unsaid, allowing him to fill in the gaps from his own imagination.

Still he didn't move. So I gave him a nudge.

'Just go Ray, go back downstairs and leave us alone before your life takes a turn for the worse.'

He looked at me, then he looked at Ivy. I felt her move further behind me from where she was now hiding. I could feel her trembling with fear. Little sobs were escaping from her with every breath she made. I wanted to turn around and cuddle her, tell her that everything was going to be okay. But first I needed Ray to go.

He looked at back at me.

'You won't tell anyone.' He stared into my eyes for a moment, then he turned and went downstairs. I heard the door slam as he went out and I hoped and prayed that he was gone for good, although in my heart, I knew he wouldn't be. Once he had stoked up on beer, he would, like the proverbial bad penny, come rolling back.

That night Ivy and I slept together in the same bed. We shoved a cupboard in front of the door, hoping it would be enough to keep him out. About midnight I heard steps coming upstairs. I hadn't heard Ray come back in, so it could only be Mum. The steps stopped outside the door.

'Amy?' I heard my mum speak through the closed and barricaded door.

Ivy was asleep by then, but I had no desire to talk to Mum. As I lay there, I could hear her sniffling. I so wanted her to come in and do what I was doing for Ivy. I needed a hug. I was just a kid and I needed some help and protection. But I knew the last person who would offer that protection would be my mum. I just couldn't trust her. After a while I heard the weeping stop, and just before she walked off down the hall, she said, 'Amy, I'm sorry.'

I didn't believe her. I still don't.

Chapter 19

Ray showed up two days later, acting as if nothing had changed. Maybe nothing had changed, but it was going to.

I had to bide my time. For a few days things were awkward. But I could see, just from Ray's looks at me and Ivy, that he was planning thinking about another move on her.

About a fortnight after the standoff, Uncle Tony rang through. He and Jo were going to a wedding reception, and their babysitter had let them down. Could Amy come over and watch Jason? My mum 'ummed' and 'aahed', but when he said he would pay me for my time, her attitude changed. She was all for more money in the family pot, especially if she didn't have to work for it herself. I insisted that Ivy had to come too. No way was I leaving her there on her own.

My mum, Ivy and I walked to Tony's. When Mum left (taking the babysitting money that was meant for me), I breathed a massive sigh of relief.

Tony and Jo were running late for their wedding reception, so they were out the door almost as soon as we had settled in. They just had time to show us the cakes Jo had made for us. I made sure to lock the door after them. Jason was still only a toddler, so he was tucked up in bed already so Ivy and I switched on the TV, grabbed the cakes from the kitchen, and settled down. We felt safer than we had done in ages. If only we could live here.

Jason normally slept okay, according to Jo but I decided I would go up and just check on him. The little lad was covered in warm blankets but was awake and grumbling a little.

I saw that his dummy had come out of his mouth. I guess when he tried to find it, he had knocked it through the bars and onto the floor. I had never dealt with a baby before and no idea of baby hygiene, so I picked the dummy off the floor and put it back into his mouth. He lifted a tiny hand to push it in properly and settled back down.

I don't think a fallen dummy did him much harm, certainly not in that clean house. Jason's bedroom floor was probably cleaner than our dinner plates at home.

I decided as I stood there in Jason's room, that when they came back, I was going to tell them. It felt like this was my big chance. It might be the only chance.

When Tony and Jo got back about eleven, I was nervous. I had been bricking it all night, ever since I'd decided I was going to tell them. I'd wavered a couple of times, but I knew inside of me that I had to do this. If I didn't take this chance, Ivy and I would suffer.

Auntie Jo was happy and giggly. She'd had a couple of drinks and a bit of a dance. Because he was driving, Tony was as sober as a judge but he seemed happy to see Jo enjoying herself.

'Come on then, kids. Let's get you home.' He looked at me as Ivy went to fetch our coats. 'What's up, Amy?' he said, frowning slightly.

I thought I was hiding it so well, but he saw through the façade immediately. Tony just put his arms around me and said nothing. He just held me tight and hugged me. Apart from Ivy, he was the only person who had touched me kindly in years.

That kindness was all I needed for everything to spill out. I started to cry. I couldn't stop myself. All of the tension, the fear, the pain, and the hatred for Tony had built up, and in a few minutes of tears and uncontrollable sobs it all came out.

It took me a while to calm down enough to speak. Then I told him everything. I told him about the drinking, the dealing, the booze, the touching, and what he had done to Ivy. I didn't mention the abortion, not in front of Ivy.

Ivy was shocked enough already to hear the story from me. Until then, she hadn't known that what had happened to her had also happened to me. Times a hundred.

When I got to the end of the story Tony was speechless. He was quiet, but trembling and breathing rapidly. I don't think I'd ever seen him angry before. I think, if I had asked him to, he would probably have killed Ray that night.

'You wait here, Amy,' he said. 'Don't worry, I just need a word with Auntie Jo.'

He and Jo went out into the kitchen for a little while. I could hear cups and spoons rattling around. I could also hear them talking. Tony was agitated while Jo kept her voice calm, despite being drunk.

When they came back in Jo looked so serious I started to feel guilty for spoiling her good mood. I'd always got on great with Jo, she seemed more like having a big sister than an aunt. I told her I was sorry for spoiling her evening. She told me not to worry, that everything would work out and there was plenty of time for fun times later. Right now, we were her concern. How did I ever doubt that Tony and Jo would be supportive?

But this was new territory for me and such a contrast to Mum. This was adults putting their own needs behind the needs of a child. We weren't used to this.

Jo sat me down on the sofa. 'What do you want to do, Amy?' I just looked at her.

'Can't we come and stay here?' I said. Ivy was looking wide-eyed.

'Oh please, *please* say yes, Auntie Jo,' she squeaked.

'Of course, you can! Darling Amy!' she said it as if she had been expecting it for ages.

Darling Amy. No one had ever called me that. Mum had never said anything so nice to me ever before. I started to cry again.

Tony and Jo looked at each other. Tony still looked angry, but he was keeping it under control.

'You can come and stay with us for as long as you like,' said Tony, 'both of you. But right now, we need to go home to talk to your mum and get your things together. When you go back in go straight upstairs and pack a few things, pants, clean clothes, toothbrushes, that sort of thing. Then I'll bring you back here and settle you into the spare room, okay? After tonight, you'll never have to go home again if you don't want to. You'll be safe here. We won't let that man near you ever again.'

I nodded. Those last few words meant so much to me. I'd dreamed of somewhere safe for a long time and now my dream was going to come true. Ivy and I would be safe. Ray couldn't hurt us anymore. I didn't think twice about leaving Mum.

When we got home, Ray told us to sneak in and get our stuff, then come back and wait in the car while he had a word with Mum. He would wait outside the door until we were out safely. It seemed like the best plan. So, with Tony standing guard outside, we crept inside and quietly shut the door behind us.

Chapter 20

In ten minutes, we were ready. We packed all my stuff first. Then, making sure no one was about, we went and packed Ivy's stuff. I was so nervous and scared to think that we were getting away. It was even better that we were getting away to someone we both knew and trusted. Other than my nan in Cornwall, there was no one else I trusted in the whole world.

I had really hoped that Mum and Ray would be asleep when we got there. But I heard movements from the living room. And as we packed, the smell of weed began percolating upstairs. My stomach was turning over and over. Ivy was sitting on the bed biting her nails. Mum and Ray were clattering around downstairs. I just wanted to run down the stairs and out the door before the arguments started.

But Tony must have got worried. Because we were halfway down the stairs with our bags, when there was a bang on the door. Not a polite knock, more of a hammering, like someone was going to kick the door in.

Ray came running out just as we reached the bottom of the stairs. He didn't see us because the hammering on the door started again.

He yelled as he pulled the door open. 'What the fuck are you doing? You'll—'

There was an almighty crack. Ray fell backwards, landing on the floor with a shout. Blood started to pour out of his nose. Uncle Tony was standing in the doorway, shaking his hand.

He nodded to us to come. As we passed the living room door, my mum stepped out. Then she saw Ray who was still conscious but flailing his arms around as if he was trying to grab something.

Tony then came in and knelt across Ray's chest. He grabbed Ray by the front of his shirt, holding his face just a few inches from his own.

'The kids told us about what's been going on here, Ray. I'm here to take them away so they're safe, but if I ever hear that you have so much as laid a finger on a kid again, I'm going to come back here and cut your knackers off. Do you get me?'

Ray didn't say anything. I think I spotted one of his brown teeth on the floor, near the door. Mum was crying and wailing, telling Tony to get off and calling him all the names under the sun.

'You!' he said, glaring up at her. 'You need to sort yourself out and clean up your life if you want to ever see those kids again. You're lucky that this is me, not the social or you would be both heading off inside. Do you understand what I'm saying, both of you?'

Ray nodded, blood pulsing from his nose.

'Good, now just in case you forget, here's a reminder.' Still holding his shirt, Tony drove his forehead into Ray's nose. There was another loud crack and blood spattered everywhere, even up the walls. Mum didn't do anything other than shout. She never tried to get Tony off, she never pounded on his back with angry fists. She never pleaded with Tony not to take us. She just complained and yelled.

'Uncle Tony?' I said. I could see that he was in danger of losing it altogether. 'Leave him now. Can we just go home?'

He looked up at me. He looked so angry, I was almost scared of him.

Finally, he let go of Ray's shirt. Ray's head bumped back onto the floor and he groaned loudly.

I walked behind Ivy as we left the house. We followed Tony out. He chucked our stuff in the boot of the car, opened the door and helped us in. That was that. We were out of there. We were out of danger.

I looked back through the rear window as we pulled away. My mum never came to the door to watch. As I looked back, I looked at the house I had been brought up in. I had spent many happy times there once upon a time, even though we lived in poverty

But the good times had been spoiled. They had been spoiled by Ray. I hated him so much for ruining that for me, and for Ivy. We never went back to live there again.

Chapter 21

My mum never did split up properly from Ray until he beat up a bouncer in a nightclub one night, after being booted out for drug dealing. Selling Ecstasy tablets to kids, he was. He beat the bouncer really badly. He got put down for dealing and GBH, and was sentenced to eight years. He came out after five years and I don't think he got in contact with Mum when he came out. Hopefully, he never will.

My mum tried her best to kick the booze and the weed but somehow, no matter how long she was off it, she always managed to slip back off the wagon and into bad habits. When she was off the booze, she became a different woman like before, but I never really trusted her again.

Ivy and I stayed with Tony and Jo right through our teens. In the summer and for Christmas, we would go down to Cornwall and see my nan. Those times down there are some of my favourite memories. As time went by, the bad memories eased and were replaced by happier times.

Tony and Jo did a magnificent job for us. I know they appreciated having us around as part of the family. But I always felt guilty that they decided not to have any more kids because we were there.

Ivy and I talked about what had happened for a while after the move away from home. I know she is grateful for what I did for her but in the end, we decided not to keep raking up the coals of bad memories and try to move on with our lives.

That is, a heck of a lot easier said than done. But she seems to be doing a fine job of it. Ivy is away at university right now. She is studying law. It turns out she was the one with brains between the two of us. I'm looking forward seeing her when she graduates. She's going to work for a big firm down in London. It's somewhere in Lincoln's Inn which sounds like a pub to me, but is apparently where all the big law firms are based.

As for me. Well, I can't honestly say I came out unscathed. I know a lot of kids that have been in the same position as me that have a lot of self-worth issues and other mental health problems. I've even heard of some girls who were so damaged physically that they were sterile, and I thank heavens I wasn't affected that way.

As soon as we went back to school I started on the extra work again, and this time, with nothing to take my mind away, my results were even better. When it came to GCSE exam times I was cacking it, so scared that I was going to fail them all. But I passed them all, except art. My childlike drawings were obviously not good enough. In fact, I ended up with eight grade A passes and a B in science. Can you believe that? I am so proud of that, I can't tell you. Tony and Jo took us all out for a meal on the day of the results to celebrate. It was fantastic.

But what was to come next? Work, training, A Levels? They were all possibilities. In the end I decided I would be better off getting a job than spending any more time at school. I'm not saying it's always a good idea to give up on education. But that was just the choice I made.

In the end, Tony came through for me again. He got me an interview at the same place he worked. It was nothing fancy, just basic office work in the beginning. But for me it was great. Working with facts and figures I'm fine, trying to be creative, not so good.

I can't believe it, but I've been there for seven years now already and I love it. Tony is still here, too. He works on the management side and I'm the credit controller. It's a great job with a decent salary. I'm so glad I worked hard at school, and also glad I didn't go on with the A Levels. I played to my strengths and it paid off.

I have my weaknesses, too, like anyone. I can't cook to save my life. No matter how many times Jo shows me, my cakes end up flat and my Yorkshire pudding remains obstinately stodgy and undercooked.

I met Dave at work, in fact he was Tony's assistant manager. He introduced us because he thought we would get along. It was amazing. We fell for each other straight away. It's like we've known each other in another life or something. And we are getting married next year. I know it's the wrong way around, but I had my first baby, Rosie, a month ago.

As I sit writing this, I often look over at her thinking I would do anything to protect her. How can that mother's love turn into the kind of selfish, 'couldn't care less' attitude of my mum?

I haven't taken Rosie to see Mum yet. I told her on the phone about the baby. I also told her straight that until she was off the booze completely, there was no way she was seeing her. I was certainly not going to be leaving Rosie with her. Ever. If you're a nan yourself, that might sound mean to you. But she is my baby and I will never, knowingly, put her in harm's way.

The biggest problem the whole affair had on me was, I suppose related to self-worth. I couldn't get past the idea in my head that somehow, even though I know intuitively that it wasn't my fault, that I could and should have done more. I'm not a great believer in therapy and psychiatrists and all that. I didn't want to relive the events over and over to try and get to the bottom of my feelings. So I haven't had any help or counselling.

For a while after we left, I was consumed with hatred, particularly for Ray and for what he did. But also for my mum and what she didn't do to protect us.

She should have protected us.

That thought would revolve in my head like the moon round the Earth. Sometimes the thought would be further away, sometimes closer, sometimes just a tiny sliver of a crescent, other times bright and luminescent, but never gone entirely. I managed to get on with my life, but those thoughts were always there.

I tried all sorts of self-help books, and some of them did help a bit. But none of them seemed to get my problem completely. I read all sorts of things to try and sort myself out. Poems, biographies, the rest of the Harry Potter books, although that was as much for pleasure as anything else.

In the end, I realised that I did not want to live my life with my insides twisted up by hatred. Life really is too short. It took time, but I have forgiven Mum and Ray now.

Because everything that happened made me who I am today. It made me all the more determined to have a different life to them. I have succeeded in that. I now have a nice life, surrounded by the people I love and who love me.

And for this, I am genuinely grateful.

More by Kate Skylark

Dirty Little Dog
Daddy's Wicked Parties
Ugly Child
Grandad's Funeral

To be first in line to hear about new books by Kate, just add your name to the mailing list. I'll let you know the moment a new book becomes available. Just write this into your browser.

http://eepurl.com/cT7DhT

You can also email kateskylark@outlook.com and ask to be added to the list.
I NEVER spam and wouldn't dream of sharing your details with anyone else.

Printed in Great Britain
by Amazon

43456239R00085